FAST FOOD

WITHDRAWN

D1462326

FOOD CONTROVERSIES

SERIES EDITOR: ANDREW F. SMITH

Everybody eats. Yet few understand the importance of food
in our lives and the decisions we make each time we eat.
The Food Controversies series probes problems created by
the industrial food system and examines proposed alternatives.

FAST FOOD

THE GOOD, THE BAD AND THE HUNGRY

ANDREW F. SMITH

REAKTION BOOKS

Published by Reaktion Books Ltd
Unit 32, Waterside
44–48 Wharf Road
London N1 7UX, UK

www.reaktionbooks.co.uk

First published 2016
Copyright © Andrew F. Smith 2016

Printed and bound in Great Britain by Bell & Bain, Glasgow

A catalogue record for this book is available from the British Library
ISBN 978 1 78023 574 5

CONTENTS

INTRODUCTION

The single most influential culinary trend of our time is fast food. It has spawned an industry that has both changed eating, the most fundamental of human activities, and created a model that works everywhere. There are 240,000 fast-food restaurants in the United States alone and a million outlets worldwide. At the heart of the industry is a score of large multinational corporations, most of which originated in the u.s. Fast-food stores are ubiquitous, located in branded stand-alone structures, urban storefronts, military bases, shopping malls, food courts, strip malls, gas stations, railway stations, airports, department stores, zoos, supermarkets and even schools and hospitals. They offer sufficiently appetizing meals at prices hundreds of millions of diverse people throughout the world can afford. Patrons need only order, gulp and go: no dressing up, no conversation, no preparation, no tipping and no clean-up.

The industry's huge global success and its high visibility have made multinational fast-food chains easy targets for a multitude of critics who voice thoughtful concerns. Appalled by the enormous effect of fast-food culture on human, animal and environmental health, critics have

published scathing exposés, supported boycotts, engaged
in demonstrations and lobbied political leaders to force
fast-food corporations to reduce the harm they cause.

The main purpose of this book is to examine controversies
related to the fast-food industry. These include the issues
surrounding the industry's globalization, the nutritional
quality and healthfulness of its food and beverages, its mass
marketing targeted at children and adolescents, its effect
on the environment and its massive influence on meat
production and on the way the industry treats its workers.

Globalization controversies are discussed in Chapter
Two. Critics proclaim that fast-food chains represent bloated
American lifestyles and the Americanization of the world's
cuisines. They fear for the survival of centuries-old local,
regional, national and ethnic cuisines. They decry the
decline of traditional restaurants and local family farms.
They also note that the fast-food industry has promoted the
industrialization of agriculture, with vast factory farms and
feedlots now dominating food production in much of the
world. Culinary leaders of the Slow Food movement have
charged the industry with 'global culinary homogenization'
and the global destruction of indigenous foodways.

Fast-food chains have come under severe criticism for the
poor nutritional quality of their offerings: highly processed
foods, many deep-fried, combined with starchy vegetables
and sugary beverages. The appeal of this food relies on the
lowest common denominators of taste: it's fatty, sweet and
salty. The fat is often highly saturated, the sugars highly
refined and the sodium levels in one meal may exceed the
recommended daily intake. Fruit and vegetables – other than

french fries – are all but absent from the menu, as are whole grains. This adds up to a shortfall in vitamins, minerals and dietary fibre. A steady diet of fast food is associated with serious health problems: obesity, Type 2 diabetes, heart disease, stroke, high blood pressure and certain cancers. Globally these medical issues have worsened in tandem with the rise of the fast-food industry. Fast food's contribution to morbidity and mortality has been a topic of concern among medical practitioners, researchers and governmental agencies around the world for three decades. The industry has responded by posting calorie counts on their websites and touting healthier menu options, but the latter seem to have limited appeal when viewed alongside double-bacon burgers and super-sized fries, and to date these lower-calorie options have had minimal impact on their customers' waistlines. Issues related to health and fast food are examined in Chapter Three.

The fast-food industry could not have achieved its vast global reach without massive marketing campaigns, particularly those targeting children and teenagers; this is the focus of Chapter Four. Hook your customers young, the theory goes, and you'll be rewarded with lifelong loyalty – and profits. Temptingly packaged kids' meals, brightly coloured toys and mesmerizing cartoon characters are central to the scheme. In-store giveaways and television advertisements on children's programmes are further lures; developing extensive in-school and school-related promotions, and opening outlets near schools, are additional snares. Chains have also been criticized for targeting low-income minority areas, resulting in higher obesity rates among children in these neighbourhoods. Fast-food chains have negotiated tie-ins with producers of children's movies and launched websites and mobile apps for kids and teenagers; the media assault is all but unavoidable. Some countries have taken steps to curtail advertising in schools and on television, but online marketing continues unabated. There's no doubt that this kind of advertising works: sales of fast food to children have skyrocketed worldwide. According to a recent study, an estimated 33 per cent of American children and adolescents eat fast food every day. The more frequently kids eat fast food, the more likely they are to be overweight or obese.

It's not just the personal health of fast-food consumers that is at risk. Chapter Five examines controversies related to the fast-food industry's effects on the environment. For decades environmentalists have charged the industry with producing excessive unrecyclable waste. The suppliers of ingredients used in fast food also come under fire: the rise in large animal feeding operations throughout the world has polluted the air, water and soil, destroyed tropical rainforests and promoted global warming. Despite mitigation measures taken by the industry and its suppliers, the overall environmental harm it has caused, directly and indirectly, continues to mount worldwide.

Animal-rights advocates, vegetarians and vegans have decried the abuse of cattle, pigs and poultry by fast-food suppliers, controversies that are covered in Chapter Six. The use of antibiotics and hormones in food animals is another global issue. The European Union banned the use of these drugs in 2007, but they are still abused in other countries.

A series of meat-related scandals has plagued the industry. These include the use of beef flavouring in McDonald's french fries, 'pink slime' in American hamburgers, horsemeat in European hamburgers and 'stinky beef' in China. Then there are widespread outbreaks of food poisoning from undercooked minced beef or employees failing to follow proper sanitation procedures. Medical professionals have long argued that we should reduce our consumption of meat, especially red meat. Those engaged in combating world hunger have long protested that the massive quantities of grain used to feed animals for fast food could be employed much more efficiently as a primary food for feeding the world today – and the world of tomorrow, which will have two to three billion more people by 2050.

A major reason for fast food's financial success has been the low wages paid to restaurant workers, millions of whom are employed at outlets and millions more at the farms and plants that supply the chains. Most fast-food workers receive the minimum wage and have no medical insurance, sick leave, family leave or childcare benefits. Their schedules are subject to the whims of their supervisors. Many workers are injured on the job and fall victim to crime because they work late into the night. In the u.s. alone 52 per cent of fast-food workers receive public assistance, costing American taxpayers an estimated $7 billion annually; ironically much of it is in the form of food assistance. Fast-food workers in the u.s. and elsewhere have begun to protest against their low wages and poor working conditions, but so far, only minimal changes have resulted. The workers employed by fast-food suppliers, such as meat-processing plants, suffer even more with off-the-clock work and on-the-job injuries; many have been maimed, and some killed, because of unsafe working conditions and an unrealistic production pace. These issues are examined in Chapter Seven.

The final chapter looks towards the future, examining the industry's options and those of its customers, and asks what society as a whole can and should do to ameliorate the major problems generated by the fast-food industry.

Before turning to the controversies, though, we should examine how the fast-food industry became so influential, the topic of Chapter One. Although many fast-food chains emerged in the 1920s, today's powerful multinational industry was launched in 1948 at one small hamburger stand in San Bernardino, California. It was called McDonald's.

1
THE BEGINNING

In 1940 two brothers, Dick and Maurice 'Mac' McDonald, opened a small drive-in restaurant in San Bernardino, California, about 60 miles east of Los Angeles. As at other American drive-ins, customers drove into the lot and parked. Carhops scurried out to greet them, hand out menus and take their orders. The orders were relayed to the kitchen; when the food was ready, the carhops delivered it on trays. When customers finished eating, the carhops gave them their bills, collected payment and carted away trays of dirty dishes.

After eight years, the McDonald brothers concluded that this system was slow, laborious and inefficient. They also had problems with employees – particularly the carhops and cooks. The young female carhops worked mainly for tips, and hence spent considerable time chatting up customers. Carhops attracted teenage boys, who were less interested in ordering food than in socializing. Cooks were often unreliable, showing up late or not at all, or coming to work inebriated. Yet another problem was customers who drove off without paying – or who pulled out of the parking lot with dishes, glasses, cups and utensils.

The brothers set about designing a better operation; then they closed their drive-in, remodelled it and reopened it on 20 December 1948. They had streamlined food preparation so that orders could be cooked quickly and assembled promptly with minimal effort, and had pared down the menu to a handful of items. The workstations were organized like an assembly line, with each employee handling simple tasks. The brothers staffed their stand with teenage boys, who were largely interchangeable – if one didn't show up, another filled in. They used only disposable paper wrappings, bags and cups, eliminating theft, breakage and cleaning. Their new model required customers to do what the carhops had done: patrons lined up at windows to place, pay for and receive their orders. They carried the meal back to the car and, after eating, threw away their own rubbish. The brothers called their new model the 'Speedee Service System'. Compared with other drive-ins, it could handle many more customers in less time at much lower cost.

Within months, their stand was serving several hundred customers daily. In 1951 the McDonalds grossed $275,000, of which $100,000 was profit, a phenomenal amount by any standard for a food-service business. Reports of the brothers' success spread around the restaurant world, and in July 1952 *American Restaurant* magazine ran a cover story on 'McDonald's New Self-Service System'.

During the next few years, the brothers continued to refine their system. They hired an architect to create a completely new building with a distinctive design that could be easily spotted from the road. It was constructed with a forward-sloping glass front; the walls were painted in red-and-white stripes. Dick McDonald came up with the idea for the 'golden arches', which bisected the roof. White tiles predominated on the walls, implying cleanliness, and there was lots of window glass, making food preparation visible to all.

The brothers advertised for franchisees, who were required by contract to build the structure that the architect had designed, follow exactly the same procedures as they proposed and offer exactly the same menu. By the end of 1953 the brothers had sold 21 franchises, only ten of which ever became operational. Compared to other fast-food chains at the time, this was an extremely modest success, but this was about to change.

Background

For millennia ready-to-eat foods have been sold on the street and from small stands throughout the world. The fare they served was inexpensive and convenient. In North America and Europe industrialization, urbanization, health laws and vendor zoning restrictions beginning in the late nineteenth century created the need for other limited-service food distribution systems for workers with extra money in their pockets. Cafeterias, buffets, luncheonettes, takeout stands and kiosks, self-service cafés, vending machines and automated cafeterias offered customers speedy service coupled with cheap food.

Fast-food chains were yet another option. They were invented in the United States during the early 1920s, and were based on efficient internal operating procedures and speedy but limited service. Compared with full service restaurants, fast-food chains were less expensive. Most specialized in one main menu item, such as sandwiches, hamburgers, hot dogs, pizza or fried chicken, accompanied by a few side orders, beverages and a dessert. Others concentrated on single items, such as ice cream, doughnuts, cookies or coffee.

Low-cost automobiles coupled with improving transportation grids created opportunities for a new type of food-service operation – the drive-in – where customers drove up to a stand, ordered food and ate in their cars. In Lodi, California, Roy Allen and Frank Wright opened their first drive-in A&W Root Beer stand in 1920. They sold food, but their signature item was a beverage – root beer. In 1924 they took an unprecedented step in food retailing: they began to franchise. For a fee, Allen and Wright supplied the root beer syrup to other drive-in operators, who were permitted to use the A&W logo, but franchisees had little else in common. The chain thrived, and by the 1950s, more than 2,000 franchise outlets sold A&W Root Beer.

Another pioneering fast-food operation was launched in 1921 by two Kansans: J. Walter Anderson, who owned three hamburger stands in Wichita, and a local entrepreneur named Edgar Waldo Ingram. They named their new operation 'White Castle'. The original menu was limited to hamburgers, coffee, carbonated drinks (sodas) and pie, but other items were added over the years. Anderson and Ingram applied the principles of Henry Ford's automobile assembly line and Frederick Taylor's views of scientific management to their food-preparation system to maximize its efficiency. Their goal was to lower costs and increase profitability.

Unlike A&W Root Beer, White Castle did not sell franchises, but it did open lots of outlets – all of them boxy white buildings with crenellated turrets. At first, Anderson and Ingram made arrangements with local butchers to supply beef ground to their specifications. As the White Castle chain grew, they established meat-processing plants, paper suppliers and bun-baking operations to ensure consistent products for all their locations.

White Castle targeted urban areas near transportation hubs or close to large factories whose workers did late-night shifts. The company used the chain-wide slogan 'Sell 'em by the sackful', and advertised widely in local newspapers, greatly increasing visibility and sales. Because its hamburgers and drinks cost mere pennies, White Castle became a little 'luxury' that many working people could afford during the Depression. In 1925 the company served 84,000 hamburgers; by 1935, it was selling 40 million a year.

The industry was abetted by the industrialization of agriculture, a process that had been under way in the u.s. since the 1920s. Thanks to mechanization and improved agricultural techniques, farmers produced cheap grain, especially wheat and corn, and inexpensive meat, particularly beef and chicken. National meat and poultry processors negotiated contracts with large food chains at greatly reduced rates. Chains passed these savings on to customers, who were drawn to fast-food by its relatively low cost. Everyone profited from this system except local eaties, small farmers and regional meatpackers who could not compete with such economies of scale.

Yet another type of fast-food operation was launched by Earl Prince, who opened an ice-cream parlour in DeKalb, Illinois, in 1926. Prince partnered with Walter Fredenhagen, his ice-cream supplier, to open a number of new outlets that were also designed to resemble castles. Their speciality was ice-cream cones and sundaes. Prince and Fredenhagen bought their paper cups from the Lily Cup Corporation. The salesman who handled the Prince Castle account was Ray Kroc, a high-school dropout who had worked for Lily Cup since 1922. Hoping to drum up more business, Kroc persuaded the partners to sell milkshakes (to be served in paper cups, of course).

Earl Prince devised an extra-thick shake consisting mostly of ice cream. Customers loved it, but it was too much for his mixer to handle. Even had the motor been up to the job, the machine could make only one milkshake at a time, and during busy times, servers couldn't keep up with orders. So Fredenhagen and Prince invented a more powerful machine, the Multimixer, with spindles that could whip up several shakes at once. It was so good that Kroc felt he could sell the new mixer to other restaurant chains, so in 1938 he left Lily Cup and established what became the Prince Castle Sales Division. Kroc promoted Multimixers at industry gatherings such as the Dairy Queen National Trade Association Convention. As he sold mixers, he also picked up the ins and outs of fast-food franchising.

When other appliance manufacturers, such as Hamilton Beach, brought out cheaper machines for making multiple shakes, sales of Kroc's Multimixer slumped. By 1954 the company was in financial trouble. It was then that the 52-year-old noticed an anomaly in one order: most outlets bought just one Multimixer, but the McDonald brothers, who owned just a single hamburger stand, ordered eight. This piqued Kroc's curiosity: why would a small hamburger stand need to make so many milkshakes simultaneously? He flew out to San Bernardino to investigate this obscure startup. The answer was simple: rather than making each milkshake as it was ordered, they prepared dozens in advance and held them in a refrigerated case. When there was a lull, shakes were prepared to refill the case. This speeded up the process of fulfilling orders.

Kroc was impressed with the operating efficiencies that the brothers had introduced. It took him just one day of observing the hamburger stand – and the crowds lined up at the front – to realize that the owners, Dick and 'Mac' McDonald, had created a system that could serve hundreds of customers promptly, efficiently and profitably. Kroc imagined that their system could easily work throughout the u.s., and he promptly negotiated an agreement with the McDonald brothers to become their exclusive franchise agent. Kroc's initial interest was not in running food stands but in selling franchises and providing Multimixers to them; this changed in 1955, when he opened his first hamburger stand in Des Plaines, Illinois.

Over the following decade, Kroc purchased the entire company from the McDonald brothers, and quickly grew the chain through franchises. He found deficiencies in the McDonald brothers' model and corrected them.

Kroc contracted with suppliers to do as much of the food preparation as possible before it arrived in outlets. Through trial and error, he created a modified fast-food model that centralized purchasing, negotiated large contracts with suppliers, developed efficient and tightly controlled internal operating procedures, hired low-cost labour, controlled franchisees tightly and launched aggressive advertising and marketing campaigns.

As ambitious and far-sighted as Kroc was, he could not have anticipated the astonishing repercussions that his creation would have on America and the world. Although his model would be tweaked and improved, virtually all successful fast-food chains – and many other businesses – have followed versions of it.

The Fast-food Industry

A robust, self-confident America emerged after the Second World War. Servicemen returned home, sought jobs, married and started families. America's war manufacturing industries turned to civilian production. Wages increased by 30 per cent during the decade following the war and disposable income increased, creating a consumer culture. Automobiles became affordable for even the working class. There were 15 million cars in 1945 in America; there were 40 million by 1950. The construction of new highways made it possible for families to move out of cities and commute by car. Low-interest, federally guaranteed home loans helped millions of veterans acquire new homes, and the postwar baby boom pushed many middle-income couples into the suburbs, which were residential tracks studded with single-family homes largely populated with baby-boom families with plenty of children. When they were first constructed, suburban neighbourhoods were devoid of eating establishments, and many entrepreneurs jumped into the culinary void. When suburban families had a little money to spare, where would they go out to dinner?

Fast-food outlets were the perfect answer to this question. Ray Kroc was one of the first to recognize the ramifications for the fast-food industry of this population shift. He refused initially to build outlets in major urban areas, which were becoming increasingly run-down and crime-ridden; instead, he selected sites in emerging suburban communities.

Fast food was particularly tempting for families with two working parents and for single parents with children.[1] Rather than spending time shopping for food, preparing it and eating at home, all they had to do was walk or drive to a fast-food outlet, place an order, grab a food-filled bag and dine. Each member of the family could choose a different combination of food and beverages. Fast food offered predictability. What was available at one chain outlet could be ordered at another and it tasted exactly the same.

McDonald's was just one of many fast-food chains in America during the 1940s and '50s. In June 1940 Sherb Noble, an ice-cream store owner in Kankakee, Illinois, acquired a franchise for selling soft-serve ice cream and opened his first outlet in Joliet, Illinois; he named the shop Dairy Queen. In 1946 Irvine Robbins and Burt Baskin opened the first Baskin-Robbins ice-cream parlours. They began selling franchises, and the chain quickly expanded.

Jack in the Box was started in 1951 by Robert O. Peterson, who offered 18-cent hamburgers at his drive-through stand in San Diego, California. In 1948 Glen Bell ran a one-man hamburger, hot dog and taco stand at San Bernardino, California; fourteen years later, he launched a chain of Mexican-inspired fast-food outlets in Downey, California, and dubbed them Taco Bell. In 1948 William Rosenberg of Quincy, Massachusetts, noting the tremendous popularity of doughnuts, opened a small doughnut shop initially called The Open Kettle. Two years later he renamed it Dunkin' Donuts and began to franchise it. Harland Sanders of Corbin, Kentucky, began franchising the secret recipe for his Kentucky Fried Chicken in 1952 and A. L. Tunick launched the Chicken Delight chain in Illinois. In Jacksonville, Florida, Keith G. Cramer opened the Insta-Burger King, later renamed Burger King. His 18-cent burgers were an immediate hit, and Cramer began franchising his operation in 1954. Four years later, Frank Carney, an eighteen-year-old student at the University of Wichita, opened a pizza parlour named Pizza Hut because the first stand looked like a hut. In 1961 Domino's pizza was created in Ypsilanti, Michigan. Many more chains were launched during the following decades. Some thrived. Those that didn't remained local favourites, went out of business or were gobbled up by the survivors.

Successful fast-food chains franchised their operation. Franchising was a system that had been applied to other businesses since the mid-nineteenth century. Typically franchisees paid franchisers an up-front fee plus a percentage on all sales. This system had several advantages: those who founded businesses could expand them without expending their own capital. Franchisees could start their own businesses by building on a successful brand without risking everything on a new venture. Ray Kroc required all McDonald's franchises to conform in every detail to his formula. This guaranteed consistency among all outlets. Other fast-food chains eventually followed Kroc's lead.

Competition among fast-food chains generated innovation: operating procedures, menus and services were regularly revised to survive in the highly competitive fast-food world. Successful chains also recognized the importance of advertising. They did so in newspapers and magazines, but the most successful promotional campaigns would be launched on television, the new medium that enthralled America in the postwar period.

Chains constantly experimented with their menus. When other fast-food chains brought out new menu items, their competitors countered with similar products. The success of Burger King's Whopper hamburger, for instance, led McDonald's to introduce Big Macs and Quarter Pounders. The popularity of KFC's fried chicken led McDonald's to come up with Chicken McNuggets, which, as observers have pointed out, are chicken only through the miracle of advertising, for they include large amounts of water, soya protein, flavourings and sugar.[2]

Other menu innovations included bundled meals (a.k.a. value meals), consisting of a preselected combination of foods such as a hamburger, french fries and a soda. Customers order by the number of the meal. Research has shown that bundled meals encourage customers to purchase more than they might if they just selected individual items.[3] It also makes it easier and less time-consuming for workers to take and assemble orders.

When one fast-food chain introduced a successful innovation, other chains followed. McDonald's began to reconsider its 'one size fits all' design when its first outlet in downtown Washington, DC, opened in 1964. There was no room for a parking lot, so indoor tables and chairs were required. Other McDonald's outlets, however, remained unchanged. When Burger King launched a newly designed restaurant with indoor seating, McDonald's management took notice. Until that time it had been assumed that people were happy to eat in their cars. But this could be uncomfortable on hot, steamy days and equally so in frigid weather. Indoor eating areas permitted year-round climate control, which Burger King customers greatly appreciated. Kroc met the challenge by developing a new restaurant with indoor seating, which McDonald's inaugurated in 1968.

Early fast-food outlets were built along highways leading into cities, and most customers arrived by car. In-N-Out Burger, a small chain based in Baldwin Park, California, installed a drive-through (more often called 'drive-thru') lane and a two-way speaker box permitting customers to order from their cars. This sped up ordering and service, and it has been a feature of In-N-Out Burger outlets ever since. During the 1950s, Jack in the Box and Burger King both experimented with a drive-through design similar to that of In-N-Out Burger. Burger King assigned separate staff to run their drive-throughs. These early efforts were unsuccessful and were discontinued.

Wendy's, a hamburger chain founded in 1969, incorporated a successful drive-through system beginning in 1971. Drive-up service windows saved space in both parking lots and indoor dining areas, as customers usually drove away and ate elsewhere. Observers credited the chain's phenomenal success to the drive-through. In response to Wendy's innovation, other chains began tearing down walls to install drive-through windows. Research showed that the windows actually increased sales. By 1976, most national fast-food chains offered the service, and some built double drive-throughs, with two traffic lanes, to speed up the delivery of orders. Outdoor menu boards were installed to further cut waiting time. Drive-through windows could stay open late, long after indoor dining areas closed. This provided protection for employees who worked late at night, as well as providing a welcome service for night-owl customers.

Drive-throughs were well received by travellers. Rather than parking, drivers picked up orders in their cars and ate while driving – or took the food elsewhere to eat. This induced car manufacturers to equip front seats with cupholders to facilitate dashboard dining. Drive-through windows featured food that could be held in one hand, enabling drivers to eat and drive simultaneously – for instance, hamburgers rather than fried chicken or pizza. McDonald's introduced its Chicken McNuggets, which were designed for easy one-handed consumption. Other fast-food operations followed McDonald's lead, and similar foods were engineered to be managed while driving. Taco Bell started using soft tortillas that would not crumble, and

KFC launched a chicken pitta sandwich; both of these could easily be held in one hand without dripping all over the eater. Eventually 78 per cent of all American fast-food sales would be from drive-throughs.[4] Speed was important for the large consumer segment known as 'functional eaters', who just want to fuel up.

For those customers too lazy to drive to a fast-food outlet, companies also offered home delivery. In the 1950s Chicken Delight in Illinois was the first company to do so. Pizza chains, such as Domino's and Pizza Hut, picked up on the idea in the 1970s. Hamburgers and french fries became soggy after preparation, but hamburger chains have now solved that problem and they do now deliver to offices and homes in selected cities around the world. In India, fast-food companies with home delivery facilities reported in 2015 that 30–40 per cent of their orders now come online, most from smartphone applications.

Another technique frequently employed by fast-food chains is 'limited time offers' (LTOs). This traditional sales technique encourages customers to buy a product now that may not be available later. LTOs permit companies to test-market new products to determine if they should be added to their regular menus. LTOs include McDonald's McRibs, which had very limited sales. In 2005 the company marketed them with a 'Farewell Tour'. The tour was a great success – and McRibs have subsequently had additional Farewell Tours. Burger King responded with its own LTO of 'real' BBQ ribs. It also introduced an LTO Sprout Surprise Whopper with a fried brussel-sprout patty and Emmental cheese in selected stores in Britain and a 'stuffed'

Steakhouse burger with bits of jalapeño peppers, cheddar cheese and condiments in the hamburger patty. From a sales standpoint, LTOS may not be financial successes, but they frequently acquire vast amounts of free advertising as news media – and Internet sources – comment on their unusual combinations.

A slightly different business strategy was developed by casual fast-food chains that emerged in the 1990s. Like other fast-food chains, fast-casual operations do not offer full table service. Customers queue to place their orders, pick up their own food, locate their own tables and throw away their rubbish when they leave. The average cost of meals at fast-casual restaurants is double that of fast-food chains, however. Fast-casual chains, such as Au Bon Pain, Boston Market, Chipotle Mexican Grill, Five Guys, Grill'd, Mad Mex, Panda Express, Panera Bread, El Pollo Loco, Qdoba, Pret A Manger and Shake Shack, focus on particular types of item, such as upscale ethnic foods, salads or bakery goods. During the past twenty years, fast-casual chains have surged throughout the U.S., and sales have regularly outpaced those of traditional fast-food outlets. In 2013 fast-casual chains grew by 11 per cent, compared with just 3.5 per cent for fast-food outlets.[5]

Fast-casual chains have attracted millennials, which bodes well for the sector's future – and not so well for traditional fast-food chains such as McDonald's, Wendy's and Burger King, which have seen declines in sales to millennials for the past seven years.[6] McDonald's have tested new upscale menu items, such as the 'Artisan Grilled Chicken Sandwich' and a premium 'Sirloin Third Pound' burger, trying to stem the exodus of younger consumers to fast casual restaurants, as yet to no avail.

Nowhere is fast-food consumption more popular than in the u.s. According to the National Restaurant Association, fast-food restaurants generated a total of $191 billion in sales during 2013 in America, where 240,000 fast-food and fast-casual restaurants served an estimated 75 million customers – about one in four Americans – every day. For many, fast food is just a beverage or a snack in addition to three meals a day. An estimated 11.3 per cent of the total calories consumed by adult Americans derive from fast food.[7] Analysts call the American industry 'mature', and most do not project high growth rates in the future. Pessimists say the industry is oversaturated, and it is increasingly difficult for franchisees to generate profits.

Optimists believe that American fast-food chains are in a period of reinvention and re-energization. Fast-food chains have begun experimenting with new upscale restaurants and new menu options. European McCafés offer a broad selection of baked goods, from brownies to doughnuts, and even cupcakes named for New York City neighbourhoods. Selected McDonald's stores have trialled table service in France, Germany, Switzerland, Austria and the UK. In Shanghai, Yum! Brands opened Atto Primo, an Italian cuisine-inspired outlet intended to test ideas for other Yum! Brands fast-food restaurants. McDonald's Australia opened The Corner, a shop to test new products and concepts for eventual rollout into their other outlets. In 2014 Starbucks launched the Starbucks Reserve Roastery and Tasting Room in Seattle to retail premium coffee.[8]

While some fast-food chains in America are stagnating, the industry is surging ahead in other countries and most multinationals are putting their energy – and their money – into expanding their operations abroad.

2
GLOBALIZATION

Until 1982 Italian laws and unions forbade the hiring of part-time employees or apprentices, who are the mainstays of fast-food chains. When the law changed, Burghy, a fast-food chain specializing in sandwiches, hamburgers and french fries, set up shop in Milan and subsequently opened additional outlets in northern Italy.

Jacques Bahbout, an Egyptian-born Frenchman who owned a coffeehouse a block from the Piazza di Spagna (at the bottom of the Spanish Steps) in Rome, was inspired by the success of Burghy and other fast-food chains elsewhere in Europe. He decided to buy a McDonald's franchise and open Italy's first American fast-food outlet. He converted his coffeehouse into the world's largest McDonald's, with a seating capacity of 450. When he opened the doors, at noon on 20 March 1986, crowds were waiting outside. By the time he closed that night, 12,350 customers had visited the restaurant, and large crowds continued to flock there for months afterwards.

The outlet's opening also drew anti-fast-food demonstrators who protested against the litter it produced, health problems associated with the type of food served, traffic congestion, noise pollution, the degradation of Rome, the

Americanization of Italy and, in the words of the Italian fashion designer Valentino, 'an unbearable smell of fried food fouling the air'.[1] The demonstrators were so deeply concerned about fast food subverting traditional Italian foodways that they distributed free pasta to passers-by.

Despite the protests, or perhaps because of them, McDonald's Italy was off to a roaring start and the chain has flourished ever since. By 2010, the company had 400-plus restaurants in Italy. When the clamour subsided, one demonstrator, Carlo Petrini, a Marxist food and wine writer, returned to his home in Bra, Italy, and founded what would become Slow Food, an international movement opposed to fast-food chains and other businesses that encourage globalization. Its mission is to protect local and regional culinary traditions, to educate consumers about the hidden risks of fast food, agribusiness and factory farms, and to promote awareness of good nutrition and wholesome food.

Background

Globalization is the increased mobility of goods, services and capital across national boundaries; it has been under way for hundreds of years. Since the Second World War, globalization's pace has quickened owing to economic and political agreements such as the World Trade Organization, the World Bank, the North American Free Trade Association and the European Union. In recent decades globalization has become more visible because of improved transportation and the advent of new technologies, especially telecommunications and the rise of the Internet.

Beginning in the late 1950s, American fast-food chains began planting their corporate flags in English-speaking countries and countries where American military units were stationed. In the process, they accumulated strengths and competencies on how to globalize their operations. They developed menu items that appealed to new customers, sourced supplies from local farmers and food processors and learned how to franchise and promote their chains. By 1975 American chains had licensed 2,379 foreign franchises, predominantly in Canada, Japan, Australia and Europe, with total sales of $875 million.[2] When the Berlin Wall fell in 1989, fast-food companies rushed into Eastern Europe.

The industry easily adapted to wealthy countries where social conditions were similar to those in the United States and there was a large potential customer base. Fast food has been particularly successful in the United Kingdom, now called the 'Fast Food Capital of Europe', where in 2002 it was reported that nine out of ten parents take their children to burger outlets.[3] McDonald's UK alone serves more than 2 million customers daily,[4] and a survey in 2014 reported that the average respondent annually downed 84 fast-food meals (including takeaways[5]), which absorbed 34 per cent of their total food budgets.[6] France, historically known for its fine dining traditions, has seen an even larger jump in fast-food consumption. Gira Cancel, a food marketing company, reported in 2013 that fast-food restaurants annually generated €34 billion and accounted for 54 per cent of the total restaurant sales in France.[7] The fast-food industry has developed at a slower but steady pace in other high-income countries.

McDonaldization and Anti-Globalization

Jim Hightower, an American small-farm activist, worried about the effect that mega-chains like McDonald's and KFC would have on agriculture and on restaurants. In 1975 he coined the pejorative term 'McDonaldization', believing that fast-food chains threatened independent restaurants and promoted the industrialization of agriculture at the expense of small family farms.[8] Hightower's fears have proven accurate in America: independent full-service restaurants have declined in number while chain fast-food outlets have ballooned upwards. In 2014, 79 per cent of all American restaurant sales occurred in fast-food chains, and only 21 per cent in traditional restaurants.[9] Simultaneously production from small family-owned farms has sharply declined, and large factory farms now dominate American agriculture.[10]

The term 'McDonaldization' was picked up and popularized in academic circles by George Ritzer, whose book *The McDonaldization of Society* (1993) examined the social effects of McDonald's success. He defined McDonaldization as 'the principles by which the fast-food restaurant' are run. These principles included efficiency, predictability and control.[11] Simultaneously Benjamin Barber popularized the term 'McWorld' (originally the name of a television promotion campaign developed for McDonald's and targeted at children) to mean the effects of globalization symbolized by the spread of McDonald's and other multinational companies around the world and the consequent destruction of indigenous cultures.[12]

To many observers, globalization has come with an American flavour, and multinational fast-food chains are visual symbols of it. Fast-food outlets are often targeted by groups that oppose American governmental or economic policies or globalization in general. In 1979 Marxist guerrillas blew up a McDonald's in San Salvador and announced that their act was intended as a blow against 'imperialist America'. In 1996 a KFC in Bangalore, India, was looted by farmers who believed that the company threatened their agricultural practices. Anarchists destroyed a McDonald's in Copenhagen in 1995. Bombs have destroyed McDonald's and other multinational fast-food outlets in Hong Kong, Brittany, Taiwan, St Petersburg, Athens, Rio de Janeiro, Xian (China), Oaxaca (Mexico) and Bali (Indonesia) – to name a few. Many other fast-food outlets have been trashed for various political reasons.

A powerful yet peaceful gesture in defiance of fast-food culture was made in 1999 by a Frenchman named José Bové, one of a group of protesters who arrived on tractors at the construction site of a McDonald's restaurant nearing completion in Millau. They methodically dismantled the prefab building, loaded up its components and deposited them in front of the local police station. Bové said that he was protesting against the 'McDomination of the world', by which he meant the standardization of taste.[13] When he went on trial, 40,000 people demonstrated on his behalf, carrying signs reading 'Non à McMerde' ('No to McShit'). Bové was convicted and served three months in a French prison. In 2000 Fausto Bertinotti, the Italian leader of the Communist Refoundation Party (Partito della Rifondazione Comunista), led an estimated 100,000 protesters to a McDonald's outlet in Rome. Bertinotti believed that McDonald's was a symbol of Americanization and globalization.[14]

U.S.-based fast-food operations have been targeted during various domestic and international crises. When American aircraft accidentally bombed the Chinese embassy in Belgrade during the war in Yugoslavia in 1999, Chinese students ransacked the McDonald's in Beijing. In the same year a petrol bomb destroyed a McDonald's in Rome because it was seen as a symbol of American imperialism.[15] During the American bombing campaign in Afghanistan in 2001, Pakistan's KFC outlets were trashed. When American and coalition forces invaded Iraq in 2003, protests were held in many cities, and multinational fast-food chains were again targeted. In 2011 the government-controlled Egyptian television station attempted to discredit the massive crowds demonstrating against the Egyptian president in Cairo: the demonstrators were unpatriotic, as evinced by their sitting in Tahrir Square dining on KFC chicken, an American food.[16] During the Ukrainian crisis in 2014, the Russian government closed several outlets of multinational fast-food chains to punish Western nations for imposing economic sanctions on Russia. The chains were reopened when their Russian workers, managers and suppliers complained. In early 2015 President Vladimir Putin announced his support for creating a 'patriotic' Russian fast-food chain to rival McDonald's and other Western chains.[17]

Emerging Nations

What is surprising is the industry's exponential surge in poorer countries, where varied and tasty cheap street food is widely available and the potential customer base for fast food is small. Hamburgers and french fries are nothing like the local fare, and fast food is a new cultural construct that includes non-food elements – new eating patterns, culinary environments and social interactions.[18] In addition, local and regional agricultural systems are often unable to supply many of the ingredients needed by fast-food chains.

Yet fast food has exploded in emerging markets in Latin America, Africa and Asia, where many potential customers associate it with status and prestige. The big push began in the 1990s. In 1991 McDonald's had a total of 1,671 restaurants in all of Latin America, the Middle East, North Africa and Asia. By 2001 the company had more than 8,800 outlets in these geographical regions, and today its outlets are found in 128 countries outside Europe.[19] In many developing countries fast-food chains are viewed as a 'modern', exotic American import.

India opened up to multinational fast-food brands in the 1990s; the chains operating there cater to the growing urban middle class. McDonald's and KFC were greeted with protests from anti-American communists and ultra-nationalists, but despite these protests, multinational chains have thrived, and Pizza Hut, Domino's, Subway, Starbucks, Taco Bell, Dunkin' Brands and Burger King, along with South African chains Nando's and Debonairs Pizza, have subsequently opened outlets. By 2013 India's more than 2,300 fast-food outlets generated an estimated $1 billion a year. Sixty-three per cent of them are global brands; indigenous chains, such as Jumboking and Goli Vadapav, are also expanding in India. In 2015 Euromonitor reported that the number of Indians consuming fast food has increased 1.7 times in the last five years.

The growth of the fast-food industry has been even more phenomenal in China. KFC opened its first outlet there in 1987; by 2013 there were more KFC outlets in China than in the U.S. During the period from 2009 to 2014 the industry expanded at an annualized rate of 12.4 per cent, reaching more than $100 billion in total sales by 2014.[20] Fast-food sales are projected to grow even faster in the future.

Glocalization

Fast food caught on in other affluent countries for many of the same reasons that the industry succeeded in the U.S. More people were commuting, more women were working and more families were eating out. Fast food was quick, cheap and convenient, and the chains were expert at advertising, particularly to children.

Fast-food multinationals learned, however, that they could not thrive in other countries by operating in the same way that they did in the U.S. Thus began the process of glocalization – working out how a global company could thrive in countries with very different political, economic, social and culinary systems. Chains generally selected in-country franchisers, who contracted with local suppliers.

In France, for instance, 80 per cent of McDonald's outlets are franchised to French entrepreneurs. All employ French managers and workers, and acquire the majority of their food and other supplies from French farmers and food processors; they import only what is necessary.

Chains also learned early on that they could not survive by selling only the menu items they offered at home. They retained some flagship items but greatly modified their menus to conform to local customs and religions, excluding items that might offend local sensibilities. In India fast-food chains do not serve beef or pork in deference to Hindus and Muslims, and they offer extensive vegetarian options. Some chains, such as KFC, maintain separate areas for preparing vegetarian and non-vegetarian dishes in India. Burger King introduced six vegetarian options, which have also been introduced into other countries. Likewise many fast-food outlets in Israel, and other countries with large Jewish populations, are kosher. Fast-food operations in Muslim countries or other places with significant Muslim populations do not serve pork and frequently use only halal meat. McDonald's restaurants in Muslim countries do not display statues of Ronald McDonald because such figures would be considered prohibited idols.

Multinational chains have also modified their practices to appeal to local culinary traditions, flavour preferences and social customs. In Rio de Janeiro McDonald's waiters serve food (with champagne) in candlelit restaurants. In Caracas, Venezuela, McDonald's hostesses seat customers, take orders and deliver meals to the tables. In South Korea

McDonald's employees seat customers at tables occupied by others during crowded times.

KFC Japan, a joint venture with Mitsubishi Trading Company, has developed special menu items such as *yaki-musubi* (grilled rice balls) to appeal to the Japanese. McDonald's China have localized their menu with offerings such as the Shrimp & Chicken Sandwich and Egg Tarts (pastry cups filled with egg custard). KFC Sri Lanka offers Chicken Buriyani (fried chicken, basmati rice and curry gravy) and Chicken Fried Rice. McDonald's Italy menu includes hamburgers (one with artichoke spread, Asiago cheese and lettuce; the other with Italian olive oil, onion and smoked pancetta); a salad (lettuce, bresaola and Parmesan cheese); and espresso. These items were tested throughout Italy before being offered in select markets in France and Switzerland as well. Chilled yoghurt drinks are on the menu at McDonald's Turkey. McHuevos (hamburgers topped with a poached egg and mayonnaise) are featured in Uruguay.

McDonald's India has offered many non-beef options including the McVeggie burger, Chicken Maharaja, McAloo Tikki (a potato-and-pea patty) and McSpicy Paneer (fresh white cheese with 'tandoori-flavored' mayonnaise). Another speciality is Shake Shake fries: the fries are served in a bag, to which the customer adds a packet of powdered hot pepper and shakes the fries to coat them. The Dunkin' Donuts menu needed major retooling in India, where American-style doughnuts did not go down well. So the franchise introduced local flavours, such as saffron, pistachios and almonds, into their doughnuts. One of the top sellers is a white chocolate doughnut topped with guava and chilli.

They also added a line of non-beef 'Tough Guy' burgers with 'fiery' sauce to their menu. KFC India introduced a 'fiery' grilled chicken to attract customers who want spicier food; Domino's offered spicy banana pizzas; Burger King created a mutton Whopper for its outlets in India.

McDonald's Japan serve a green-tea flavoured milkshake and Teriyaki McBurgers, which are also on the menu in Taiwan and Hong Kong. Samurai Pork Burgers were once featured in Thailand. The McRice, a burger with rice, is offered in Indonesia. A burger with a fried egg and sliced beetroot, called the Kiwiburger, is a big seller in New Zealand, and grilled salmon sandwiches – McLaks – are served in Norway. The McPepper offered in Singapore has a black pepper sauce. Customers in Athens can order a Greek Mac served in pitta bread with yoghurt sauce. Beer is served at fast-food chains in Germany, and wine in France.

Other fast-food chains have made similar adaptations and concessions to their surroundings. In Singapore, Japan and Thailand, Starbucks offered a Caramel Coffee Jelly Frappuccino to appeal to the local taste for jellied desserts. Nacho Whoppers (burgers with nacho chips, jalapeños and a Mexican sauce) are available at Burger King outlets in the Netherlands. In 2010 Burger King Dubai introduced a six-serving Pizza Burger (cut into wedges for sharing) made with tomato sauce, pepperoni and cheese. In Japan Burger King has introduced a technology called the 'Musical Shower', which permits diners to listen without earphones to their own music (without bothering those seated nearby) through the use of a domed speaker over each table. Baskin-Robbins adapted its menu to Japanese tastes with ice-cream flavours such as Popping Shower (white chocolate and crème de menthe flavour, studded with popping candy), matcha (green tea) and muskmelon.

Indigenous Multinational Chains

Simultaneous with the expansion of multinational fast-food chains has been the rise of indigenous chains that modelled themselves on American fast-food operations. Chains took off in Canada for the same reasons as in the United States. Tim Hortons, a Canadian doughnut and coffee chain, opened its first store in Hamilton, Ontario, in 1964. Its eponymous founder was a professional hockey player. In addition to its original offerings, the chain now serves soups, sandwiches and breakfast items. In 2014 Tim Hortons had 5,000 locations in Canada, the U.S. and the Middle East; it is now a division of Restaurant Brands International, which is owned by 3G Capital Partners, a financial investment firm based in Brazil. Restaurant Brands also owns Burger King and is in the process of relocating its international headquarters from Miami to Canada.[21]

By 2006 more than 2,600 other fast-food brands were operating in Canada.[22] Manchu Wok, which serves familiar Chinese-restaurant fare, now has outlets in the United States. It is the largest chain of Chinese fast-food restaurants in North America. Extreme Pita, a Canadian chain launched in 1997 by Alex and Mark Rechichi, who wanted to offer more healthful fast food, serves Middle Eastern-style pocket breads filled with steak, chicken, deli meats, salads, falafel or vegetables. It now has outlets in several U.S. states. Teriyaki

Experience, a Japanese-style chain, first opened in Canada in 1986. Offering teriyaki meats, seafood, tofu and vegetables, this chain also serves Japanese noodle dishes and dumplings. Teriyaki Experience has more than 100 outlets in Canada and the United States.

Headquartered in London, the sandwich and salad chain Pret A Manger (*prêt à manger* is French for 'ready to eat') was launched in 1984; as of 2015 it operates more than 300 outlets in the United Kingdom, and an additional 100 in Hong Kong, Singapore and the u.s. London-based PizzaExpress, founded in 1965, has more than 400 outlets in the UK and additional locations in Europe, the Middle East and South Asia. YO! Sushi opened its first restaurant in London in 1997, and now also operates in the Middle East, Russia, Ireland and the United States.

Maoz, a small vegetarian falafel chain that originated in the Netherlands in 1996, has locations in Europe, North America and Australia. The Belgian hamburger chain Quick, which set up shop in Antwerp in 1970, is now the largest fast-food chain in Belgium and Luxembourg, and the second largest in France. (McDonald's is the largest fast-food chain in France, with more than 1,000 outlets.)

In South Korea the Paris Croissant Company operates a chain of bakeries and limited-service cafés called Paris Baguette. Today it is the largest fast-food chain in Korea and has outlets in China, Vietnam, Singapore and the United States. Jollibee Foods started as an ice-cream parlour in Quezon City, Philippines, in 1975. Three years later, owner Tony Tan Caktiong and his Chinese-Filipino family expanded their offerings to include baked goods, sandwiches, the Yumburger (a hamburger) and later Chickenjoy and Jollibee Spaghetti. They opened additional shops in the Manila area and incorporated Jollibee Foods. Today the conglomerate is the largest fast-food chain in the Philippines, with about 1,600 outlets offering hamburgers, fried chicken, spaghetti, noodles, rice-based meals and dishes made with Spam. The company has opened hundreds of outlets under various names in China, Guam, Saipan, Vietnam, Taiwan, Hong Kong, Saudi Arabia, Dubai, Qatar, Kuwait, Malaysia, Brunei and Singapore. In 1988 Jollibee opened its first franchise in the u.s. and has opened many subsequently.

In Japan mos Burger (its name is an acronym of 'Mountain Ocean Sun') opened its doors in 1972, the year after McDonald's arrived in the country. Its founders conducted a careful study of how McDonald's was run – and then did exactly the opposite. Instead of cranking out quick, cheap hamburgers, mos Burger emphasized the quality and safety of its ingredients. By 2014 there were more than 1,700 mos Burger outlets in Australia, Hong Kong, Indonesia, Singapore, South Korea, Taiwan and Thailand.

El Pollo Loco ('the crazy chicken') first opened in Guasave, in the state of Sinaloa, Mexico, in 1975; the chain expanded to northern Mexico and, in 1980, opened its first outlet in Los Angeles. The menu featured flame-grilled marinated chicken, as served across much of Latin America and also popular with Latinos in the United States. El Pollo Loco has expanded its menu to include burritos, tacos, salads and other Mexican-style dishes. It now has almost 400 outlets in the United States.

Pollo Campero, launched in Guatemala in 1971, is now the largest fast-food chicken chain in Central America. In 2002 Pollo Campero franchised a restaurant in Los Angeles, its first in the United States. The chain has now expanded to several states and also has outlets in Europe, the Middle East and Asia.

In South Africa Nando's, launched in 1987, features the flavours of Mozambique, the small neighbouring country that was colonized by the Portuguese. Their signature offering is flame-grilled chicken marinated with local peri-peri chillies, but they also serve burgers, pitta sandwiches, salads, chicken wings and wraps. Nando's has more than 1,000 outlets in 28 countries in Africa, Asia, Europe, the Middle East, Oceania and North America. Another South African fast-food company, Steers (now Famous Brands), got its start in 1970 and today is the largest hamburger chain in South Africa. It has more than 500 outlets, with franchises in Botswana, Ivory Coast, Kenya, Mauritius, Swaziland, Tanzania, Zambia and Zimbabwe, as well as in the UK. Famous Brands also owns Debonairs Pizza, with 500 outlets in 2014. Debonairs is the largest pizza chain in Africa and also has locations in India and Dubai.

Mr Bigg's, a Nigerian fast-food brand specializing in meat pies, jollof rice and moin moin (a steamed bean pudding), originated as a department-store coffee-shop chain; it was re-created as 'Mr Bigg's' in 1987, and today has almost 200 outlets in major cities in Nigeria and Ghana. Following in Mr Bigg's footsteps are Tantalizers and Tastee Fried Chicken, smaller chains that specialize in hamburgers, chicken and meat pies. In all there were 70 fast-food brands operating in Nigeria in 2008.[23]

In Zimbabwe, Innscor International Franchising was launched in 1987; it owns several different chains with more than 300 outlets that variously sell hamburgers, pizza, chicken and bakery goods in Ghana, Kenya, Malawi, Mauritius, Nigeria, Senegal, Tanzania, Uganda and Zambia.

These are just a few of the non-American fast-food chains that have expanded beyond their countries of origin. Today, the total number of fast-food chain outlets in the world is conservatively estimated at 1 million, and chains are rapidly continuing their global expansion. All projections point to an even greater global surge in the fast-food business in the future.

Positive and Negative Effects

In communities where fast-food chains are common, small cafés and restaurants are often unable to compete. The chains are perceived as a cultural threat to traditional cuisines, and have become a symbol of American cultural imperialism. McDonald's, Subway, Domino's and KFC offer 'foreign' delicacies, such as 'American' hamburgers, pizza, fried chicken and french fries, that take market share from indigenous food producers. To forestall potential criticism, fast-food chains have done their best to localize their operations. Most in-country multinational chains are owned wholly or in part by nationals. Most outlets are operated by nationals, and the chains generally purchase a large percentage of their basic ingredients from local farmers, importing only necessities that are not available locally.

Several factors account for the success of multinational fast-food operations. They possess cutting-edge technology and employ innovative strategies to attract customers, prepare and serve food, and keep their operations profitable. Local entrepreneurs have benefited by partnering with multinational fast-food chains as franchisees or suppliers. Working closely with multinational chains, these entrepreneurs learn state-of-the-art technology, professional techniques and sophisticated business practices.

In poorer countries fast food is seen as a luxury, to the point where wedding receptions, birthday parties and other celebrations are sometimes held at fast-food restaurants. Fast food is considered an exotic import symbolizing fun, modernity and connectedness; the familiarity of chain outlets offers a sense of safety and sanctuary. In more affluent countries chains appeal to busy, upwardly mobile, middle-class urbanites with limited time to dine. Customers are attracted to fast food's convenience, efficiency, reliability, predictability and cleanliness (including their all-important toilets). Around the world, the industry has created jobs for unskilled workers at salaries higher than those at comparable stand-alone restaurants.

This incredible global success has come at a very high price for many of the industry's best customers and for the public health services where fast-food chains thrive. If fast-food chains continue to grow at their current pace, within a few decades people in low- and middle-income countries will be consuming as much fast food as those in richer countries, and will face the same weight and health problems that confront frequent customers in more affluent areas. The fare served at fast-food chains is typically high in calories, fat, sugar and sodium, so it comes as no surprise that frequent fast-food consumption is associated with overweight, obesity and many other chronic diseases – topics to which we now turn.

3
HEALTH

The most distinctive item sold at McDonald's during its early years wasn't their cheap burgers – it was their french fries, served hot, crisp and salty-sweet. The McDonald brothers used Russet Burbank potatoes bought from a single source. Employees peeled, cut and deep-fried them at intervals throughout the day to make sure the fries were always hot and fresh. McDonald's french fries were praised by virtually everyone, from their earliest local customers to American culinary icons like James Beard and Julia Child.

McDonald's fries generated more profit than their burgers. As the chain began to grow in the 1960s, dozens of different suppliers were contracted to supply regional outlets, and the uniformity and quality of McDonald's french fries suffered as a result. In 1965 Ray Kroc, the chain's chief executive officer, met the Idaho potato grower J. R. Simplot, owner of the Simplot Potato Company: the french-fry world has never been the same since. Working with Simplot scientists, McDonald's researchers devised ways of freezing raw, precut fries without compromising their quality. Employees had only to drop the prefabricated frozen potato sticks into the basket of a deep-fryer; that appliance kept the oil at a precise temperature, and a buzzer alerted the operator when the fries were done. This system eventually shaved 30 to 40 seconds off the delivery time. Multiplied by the millions of customers ordering fries, the time saved covered the equipment costs and generated huge profits. Just as important to Ray Kroc was the fact that this process meant that french fries served at any McDonald's location in the United States would taste exactly the same. While other chains bought the same frozen potatoes and employed similar equipment, their french fries never tasted quite as good as the ones from McDonald's.

In 1984 Bonnie Liebman, Director of Nutrition for the Center for Science in the Public Interest (CSPI), a Washington-based nonprofit, found something unexpected when she analysed french fry samples from various fast-food chains. She discovered that McDonald's fries were high in cholesterol – something that's not naturally present in vegetables. The reason, she discovered, was that McDonald's fried their potatoes in fat that was 93 per cent beef tallow (rendered fat) and 7 per cent soy oil. At first, it was the beef fat that gave the fries their distinctive flavour – and their cholesterol. McDonald's french fries were also very high in sodium. Liebman wrote exposés for the CSPI's *Nutrition Action HealthLetter* and the CSPI launched a campaign to stop McDonald's using highly saturated, cholesterol-laden animal fat for frying. The CSPI also urged the chain to reduce the amount of added salt in its french fries.

Today the unique taste of McDonald's french fries has nothing to do with the type of potato, the technology that processes them or the equipment or oil that fries them. What gives McDonald's fries their unique taste is the chemical flavourings that are added to the oil. The beef tallow has been replaced with taste enhancements, colourings and sweeteners produced by the flavour industry.[1]

Fast-food french fries have few nutritional benefits other than calories,[2] but thanks to advertising targeting youth and a tasty menu item, 25 per cent of the total vegetables consumed by American children are in the form of french fries.[3]

Background

The main objective of any restaurant is to entice customers to order food and drink – and encourage them to return. Fast-food purveyors learned early on that their customers were most attracted to menu items that were salty, fatty or sweet – or, if possible, all three. Researchers later concluded that the vendors were right: human brains are hardwired to crave fat, salt and sweetness. The really good news for fast-food chains was that sugar, sodium and fat are very inexpensive ingredients.

Fast-food recipe developers have used this knowledge to formulate menu items with optimal appeal: sugar, fat and salt are coupled with numerous flavourings and chemical additives. Milkshakes, ice cream-like menu items, and doughnuts, for instance, are both sugary and fatty. French fries, hamburgers, onion rings, fried chicken and pizza depend on plenty of fat and salt for flavour. To bring together all three key factors, hamburger buns and pizza crusts got sweeter with the addition of high-fructose corn syrup. Even fries were sprayed with a sugar solution (which also helps to crisp and brown them). The ketchup that customers slather on their fries is also sweet. Chicken menu items also have added sugar. McDonald's Southern Style Chicken Breast contains sugars, salt, starch and artificial flavourings – and that is before being dipped in batter. KFC's fried chicken is battered with a mixture that includes flour, salt, sugars, corn syrup and flavourings. And of course, fried chicken is cooked in plenty of fat. Salad dressings and 'special sauces' have a strong note of sweetness. With fat, sodium and sugar as common denominators, most fast-food menu items were (and are) high in calories and low in dietary fibre, vitamins and minerals (other than plenty of sodium).

Concern about the nutritional content of fast food began in 1984 with Marion J. Franz, the Director of Nutrition at the International Diabetes Center in Minneapolis. Her *Fast Food Facts* (1983) examined the nutritive value of menu items and she made recommendations for diabetics on what to eat – and what not to eat – at national fast-food chains.

A more systematic approach was taken by the CSPI, which began to seriously examine the nutritional composition of fast-food menus and assess the potential health consequences of eating fast food. Michael Jacobson and Sarah Fritschner's *The Fast-Food Guide* (1986) analysed the nutrients in foods served at major fast-food chains. For each item, calories, fat, saturated fat, cholesterol, sodium, sugar and additives were published – information that the companies themselves did not want to share with the public. They decried the high fat, saturated fat, sugar and sodium contents of fast-food meals and despaired of their effect on public health. *The Fast-Food Guide* was the first significant exposé of fast-food formulas, and ignited interest in exploring the health consequences of eating fast food. The CSPI popularized the term 'empty calories', meaning foods and beverages with plenty of fat, sugar and calories, but little or no vitamins, minerals and other micronutrients.

Soda

One fast-food menu item that fell into the empty calorie category was sugary carbonated drinks (sodas), which Michael Jacobson, the CSPI's executive director, called 'liquid candy'.[4] Beginning in the 1970s, soda companies saw fast-food chains as a way to build sales for their beverages. PepsiCo acquired several fast-food chains, including Pizza Hut, Taco Bell and KFC. All these chains sold soft drinks manufactured by PepsiCo. In 1997 PepsiCo divested itself of its restaurant subsidiaries, creating a separate corporate entity now called Yum! Brands. PepsiCo maintained the largest ownership in Yum! Brands. Consequently Yum! Brands' fast-food companies continued to sell Pepsi beverages. Coca-Cola entered into agreements with competing chains, including McDonald's. Soda companies convinced fast-food chains that they could draw in more customers with 'combo meals' that included a main dish, a side order (such as french fries) and a soft drink. These and other promotional efforts did attract customers, and soda sales soared in the 1990s.

Low ingredient costs, high profits and intense competition for market share encouraged fast-food chains to sharply increase soda portion sizes. Fast-food chains upped soda sizes from 8 ounces (236 ml, 90 calories) to 12 ounces (140 calories) to 32 ounces (354 ml, 310 calories) to 64 ounces (1.89 litres, 610 calories), and many outlets offered free refills. Soda from all sources (home consumption, fast-food chains, vending machines and restaurants) is estimated to be the source of 7–9 per cent of the total calories that Americans consume, and soda is the primary source of added sugars in the American diet.

In June 2012 Michael Bloomberg, the mayor of New York City, proposed a cap on the sale of sugary drinks supplying more than 25 calories per 8 fluid ounces. The proposal did not survive a court challenge, but had it gone into effect, it would have been illegal for the city's fast-food outlets, cinemas and food trucks to sell sodas larger than 16 ounces (473 ml). Customers, of course, could have bought more than one soda, and this ban would not have affected sugary soft drinks sold in convenience or grocery stores. Researchers concluded that such a cap would have cut 63 calories from the average fast-food meal.[5]

Fast-food chains in other countries have also increased their beverage sizes. In France Quick and KFC installed free soda refills as well. Evidence emerged that this initiative fuelled a 10 per cent increase in the quantity of soda consumed. In 2015 French officials voted to ban unlimited soda refills at restaurants and fast-food chains nationwide.[6]

Supersized

Soft drinks are not the only fast-food offering that
have got bigger. Burgers have ballooned from a 1-ounce
(28-gram) patty in 1957, with a few hundred calories,
to the 1997 half-pound (227-gram) hamburger (or a
double quarter-pounder) with 750 calories. In Japan the
McDonald's Mega Tamago, a variation on the Double Big
Mac, has more than 1,000 calories. A Carl's Jr. half-pound
Guacamole Bacon Thickburger supplied 1,210 calories
along with 89 grams of fat and 1,910 milligrams of sodium.
A Hardee's Monster Thickburger weighed in at 1,290 calories,
92 grams of fat and 2,840 milligrams of sodium. (The Double
Donut Burger sold at Hungry Horse, a pub-restaurant chain
in England, Wales and Scotland, had 1,996 calories.) Add a
side of fries and a shake to the above burgers and a single
fast-food meal could easily add up to more than a total day's
worth of calories, fat and sodium prescribed for adults.[7]

In the 1950s a standard portion of fries at McDonald's
was a modest 2½ ounces (71 g) and had about 230 calories.
The chain subsequently added a medium portion of fries
– about 4 ounces (113 g), with about 340 calories – and a
large, about 6 ounces (170 g), with a little over 500 calories.
In 1994 McDonald's added 8-ounce (227 g) 'Super Size'
fries to their menu – with 800 calories and 29 grams of
fat, more than triple the size of the original serving. The
company also offered supersized meals, consisting of a
burger or other sandwich, supersized fries and a supersized
beverage (42 ounces or 1.24 litres), which averaged in
total about 1,500 calories – 75 per cent or more of the

recommended adult daily calorie intake. (To burn off the calories in this combination, one would have to walk for about seven hours straight.) Signs at McDonald's outlets encouraged customers to 'Super Size It!' and order-takers were required to ask customers if they wanted to supersize their order. A supersized meal cost less than the three items ordered individually, but McDonald's still made higher profits on each supersized order.

The term 'supersized' was adapted for use in many other retail establishments, and fast-food chains created their own names for extra-large portions. Burger King's, naturally, were called 'King Size'. The reason for the tremendous success of supersized meals was simple: most people when eating out want value for their money. A much larger portion for just a little more cash looks like a good deal. This might well be a good option if two people were sharing the supersized meal, or if the customer ate a reasonable amount and took the leftovers home for another meal. But people typically clean their plates, which is precisely what our mothers always taught us to do. A fascinating study in 2005 suggested that many people are not aware of how much they have eaten. They eat until the food on the plate is gone – ignoring physical cues telling them that they are full.[8] Dr David Kessler, former Surgeon General of the United States and the author of *The End of Overeating* (2009), concluded that many people are afflicted by 'conditioned hypereating', an intrinsic drive to eat beyond what they need.[9]

In 2004 the film *Super Size Me* was released. Written and directed by Morgan Spurlock, a New York-born journalist and filmmaker, the film documented a four-week period during which Spurlock ate nothing but McDonald's food. Over the 28 days he gained 24 pounds (10.9 kg), suffered from depression and developed liver problems. While the film has its weaknesses, the relationship between increased portion size, calorie intake and weight gain is clear.[10] It was also a public relations nightmare for McDonald's, who stopped offering supersized meals and beverages a few months before the film debuted. (Company representatives claimed that the decision had nothing to do with the film, but that seems most unlikely.) Other fast-food chains, however, have had no problem continuing to sell gargantuan portions of food and drink. A 2015 u.s. Department of Agriculture-funded study of three fast-food chain menus concluded that there had been little change over eighteen years regarding portion sizes and the calorie, sodium, saturated fat and trans fat content of popular meal combos. It comes as no surprise that increased consumption of fast foods and beverages are associated with weight gain and obesity.

Obesity

According to studies published in 2011 in the prestigious British medical journal *The Lancet*, the global prevalence of obesity has almost doubled since 1980, 'when 4.8 percent of men and 7.9 percent of women were obese.'[11] In 2014 the World Health Organization (who) estimated that 'more than 1.9 billion adults, 18 years and older, were overweight. Of these, more than 600 million were obese.'[12] The numbers are increasing in nearly every country in the world. Excess weight and obesity results in higher rates of chronic diseases, including high blood pressure, arthritis, infertility, heart disease, Type 2 diabetes, strokes, birth defects, gall-bladder disease, gout, an impaired immune system, liver disease, osteoarthritis, sleep apnoea and several types of cancer (including breast, prostate, oesophageal, colorectal, endometrial and kidney cancer). It comes as no surprise that obese individuals have a 50 to 100 per cent increased risk of premature death from all causes compared with those who are at normal weights.[13]

The obesity crisis in America is acute. During the past 50 years, obesity rates have been rising, such that today 61 per cent of Americans are classified as overweight. u.s. obesity rates have risen from 12 per cent to 20 per cent of the population since 1991. Of particular concern has been weight gain among children. Over the past three decades, the obesity rate has more than doubled among preschool children and adolescents in the United States, and has tripled among all school-age children. Obesity now affects about 12.5 million American children. According to standards established by the International Obesity Task Force, 35 per cent of American children are overweight or obese. Research indicates that an overweight child has an 80 per cent chance of becoming an obese adult. The medical costs of dealing with diseases associated with obesity and overweight are high: the u.s. spent $210 billion treating obesity-related illnesses in 2010; by 2030 obesity-related healthcare costs are expected to hit $550 billion.

There is no single cause of obesity; genetics, environment and activity levels all play a role, but by definition people gain weight by consuming more calories than they expend. The rise in obesity correlates with the growth of the fast-food industry, which has made inexpensive, calorie-dense, high-fat foods universally available. Eating more fast-food meals usually means consuming more calories, fat and salt, and fewer fruits and vegetables. Studies have shown that fast-food meals on average contain 70 per cent more calories than meals eaten at home.[14]

Eating more than two fast-food meals a week has been linked to significantly more weight gain than occasional consumption.[15] A WHO study concluded that fast-food consumption was a predictor of weight gain.[16] The Centers for Disease Control and Prevention (CDC) examined the eating habits of Americans and concluded that 12.8 per cent of the total calories consumed by adults derived from fast food. The good news is that the total daily fast-food calories consumed by American adults have declined to 11.3 per cent of all calories consumed, a significant drop. For those aged 20 to 39, however, fast food accounted for more than 15 per cent of their daily calories. The percentage of total daily calories from fast food increased as weight increased. Obese young adults acquired 18 per cent of their daily calories from fast food.[17]

Cheeseburger Laws

In the wake of the successful lawsuits against tobacco companies in the 1990s, overweight Americans filed lawsuits against fast-food giants, claiming that eating their food and drinking their beverages caused their diabetes, high blood pressure and obesity. In July 2002, 56-year-old Caesar Barber, who weighed 270 pounds (122 kg), was the lead plaintiff in a class-action suit against McDonald's, Burger King, KFC and Wendy's, alleging that the restaurants were responsible for the plaintiffs' poor health. Another class-action suit, this time with two obese teenagers as plaintiffs, went after McDonald's in 2003. That suit, *Perlman et al. v. McDonald's Corporation*, alleged that the chain's food had caused the youngsters to become obese, and that the company engaged in deceptive advertising and fraud, among other things. The charges accused McDonald's of selling food that was harmful, and of being negligent in informing its customers of the danger. The Perlman lawsuit was dismissed, refiled and finally dismissed again in 2010: the judge's decision was that the plaintiffs had not shown a clear cause and effect relationship between eating a particular company's food and obesity.

Lawsuits like *Perlman et al. v. McDonald's* and *Monet Parham v. McDonald's* (2010) encouraged states to pass legislation to prevent people from suing fast-food restaurants or food manufacturers on grounds that their food is to blame for causing obesity or related illnesses such as heart disease, diabetes or hypertension. In June 2003 Louisiana was the first state to pass what was called a cheeseburger law, and subsequently at least eighteen other states have passed such laws. Similar bills have been introduced in other state legislatures.

Fortune magazine asked on the cover of its 3 February 2003 issue: 'Is Fat the Next Tobacco?' To date, the answer is no. Unlike tobacco, whose nicotine and tar are addictive and clear contributors to lung and other diseases, fast food is diverse – from burgers to salads to french fries to soda to coffee to doughnuts to ice cream. People eat fast food regularly and do not become obese, and many people who are obese do not eat fast food. No clear cause and effect relationship has been established, as it has been with tobacco and lung cancer.

Location and Obesity

Many studies have examined the connection between the location of fast-food outlets and obesity in the surrounding areas. A systematic review of these studies in 2011 found that fast-food restaurants were more prevalent in low-income areas and that higher body mass index was associated with living in areas with increased exposure to fast food.[18] Subsequent studies in several countries have confirmed that fast-food outlets near homes, work and commuting environments are associated with greater body mass index. People with the greatest exposure to fast-food outlets were almost twice as likely to be obese.[19] Several studies have suggested that zoning restrictions be placed on fast-food restaurants near low-income residents.[20]

In 2008 the Los Angeles City Council enacted a moratorium on the construction of new stand-alone fast-food restaurants in a 32-square-mile (83-square-kilometre) area in South Los Angeles, a low-income neighbourhood. They found that there were already 1,000 fast-food restaurants in this area, a far greater concentration than elsewhere in the city. They also found that 30 per cent of the 750,000 residents in the area were obese, double the rate in more affluent parts of the city. In 2015 the Rand Corporation found that obesity rates in South Los Angeles continued to rise after passage of the ban. Before the fast-food ordinance went into effect, 63 per cent of South Los Angeles residents reported being overweight or obese; three years later, 75 per cent reported being overweight or obese. Advocates for the ban responded by stating that they never thought the ordinance was a 'silver bullet' for solving obesity. They claimed instead that goal was to create more options for residents in South Los Angeles.[21]

Type 2 Diabetes and Other Diseases

Worldwide, the number of people with diabetes has increased from an estimated 153 million in 1980 to almost 350 million in 2011. The Centers for Disease Control has projected that one-third of American children will develop diabetes in their lifetime. It is a preventable disease that reduces life expectancy by several years. The most common form is Type 2, also called 'adult onset' diabetes as it was formerly rare in children. However, Type 2 diabetes is 'increasingly diagnosed in youth and now accounts for 20% to 50% of new-onset diabetes case patients, disproportion- ately affecting minority race/ethnic groups', according to a 2014 research study published in the *Journal of the American Medical Association.*[22]

Studies have linked eating fast food with Type 2 diabetes and other diseases. Researchers at the University of North Carolina studied the eating habits of 3,643 young adults over a thirteen-year period, and concluded that 'Those who ate the most fast food weighed more, had larger waists and triglyceride levels, and showed signs of metabolic syndrome – a precursor to diabetes, heart disease and possibly cancer.'[23]

As fast-food chains have planted their flags in various countries, several studies have associated increases in fast-food consumption and Type 2 diabetes. A study published in 2005 in *The Lancet* examined the health and eating habits of 3,031 young adults who were 18–30 years old in 1985, and then followed them over a fifteen-year period. The authors concluded that 'Fast-food consumption has strong positive associations with weight gain and insulin resistance, suggesting that fast food increases the risk of obesity and type 2 diabetes.'[24]

A study by researchers at Australia's Garvan Institute of Medical Research concluded that the increase in Type 2 diabetes in Ho Chi Minh City, Vietnam, was caused by changing lifestyles, including fast-food consumption.[25] An examination of Chinese Singaporeans in 2012 concluded that 'Western-style fast food intake is associated with increased risk of developing type 2 diabetes mellitus and of coronary heart disease mortality in an Eastern population.'[26]

Fast-Foodborne Illnesses

Foodborne illnesses have many causes. Fifty years ago the main culprit was improper handling or storage of food. Generally those outbreaks affected only a limited number of people in a particular area. But with increased industrialization and centralization of food systems, a problem anywhere in the food chain has the potential to explode into a crisis. As fast-food operations serve millions of customers daily, it comes as no surprise that some have been sources of outbreaks of foodborne illness.

Eric Schlosser, author of *Fast Food Nation: The Dark Side of the All-American Meal* (2001), pointed to a major cause of this increase in foodborne disease: the vast expansion of the meatpacking industry in response to increased demand from fast-food chains. Schlosser estimated that each year roughly 100,000 Americans, mainly children and the elderly, are sickened by *E. coli* bacteria. Indeed, outbreaks of the potentially deadly *E. coli* 0157:H7 have been traced to meat processors' operations, just as *Salmonella* has increasingly been traced to poultry processing plants. A USDA study reported in 1996 that 7.5 per cent of the samples taken at processing plants were contaminated with *Salmonella*; 11.7 per cent were contaminated with *Listeria monocytogenes* (of which one in five cases proves fatal), 30 per cent with *Staphylococcus aureus* and 53 per cent with *Clostridium perfringens*; 78.6 per cent of ground beef contained *E. coli* (Biotype 1) – microbes that are indicators of faecal matter.[27]

Meat processing has changed over the past 50 years. A hamburger bought in 1970 would probably have contained meat from a single steer or cow. Today, a fast-food hamburger patty may contain meat from 1,000 cows that have been raised in five different countries. Using meat from many animals increases the chances that the hamburger will be contaminated with bacteria. According to the USDA, contaminated meat causes 70 per cent of all foodborne illnesses.[28] The Food Safety and Inspection Service (FSIS), a branch of the U.S.

Department of Agriculture (USDA), has tested more than 26,000 samples of ground beef since 1996. Of these, 25 tested positive for *E. coli* and none was associated with any outbreak of illness. Recently FSIS inspections of meat-processing plants have increased, and incidences of *E. coli* have decreased.

Foodborne illnesses have been traced to fast-food outlets. In January 1993 Jack in the Box distributed hamburger patties contaminated with foecal matter to its Pacific Northwest restaurants. Patties were served undercooked, and the surviving *E. coli* O157:H57 bacteria in the meat caused 600 customers to become ill; four children died. The company was served with hundreds of lawsuits, most of which were settled out of court. A nine-year-old girl who suffered kidney failure received $15.6 million. In addition to its legal costs, the company lost $44 million in sales, largely because of the bad publicity. It sued the supplier, Vons Companies of Arcadia, California, that had sent the contaminated meat to the company's restaurants. The lawsuit was settled in 1998; Vons paid Jack in the Box's parent company, Foodmaker, $58.5 million. Jack in the Box changed its policies and procedures to avoid future problems.

The Taco Bell distribution centre in New Jersey was the likely source of an *E. coli* O157:H7 outbreak in 2006. Taco Bell was also tied to other *Salmonella* outbreaks in 2010 and 2011.[29] Employees who failed to wash their hands properly were the most probable vector of these illnesses. In 2009, 32 people, including two workers, were confirmed to have contracted hepatitis A after eating at a McDonald's restaurant in Milan, Illinois. Hepatitis A is transmitted through faecal matter, and it is likely that employees did not follow proper sanitation procedures.

These are a few of the known cases in which fast-food outlets have been involved. In most cases the actual source of the foodborne illness is not determined. The CDC estimates that 48 million Americans – about one in seven – become ill from these illnesses every year. Of these, 128,000 are hospitalized and 3,000 die. The CSPI traced 44 per cent of foodborne illnesses to restaurants in general.[30]

Fast-food Addiction?

Addiction is defined as the persistent, compulsive use of a substance regardless of its negative consequences. The addictive effects of alcoholism, drug abuse and chain smoking are well documented. Foods that contain large amounts of sugar, fat and sodium, such as most offerings at fast-food chains, have been specifically identified as potentially addictive. Sugar, fat and sodium stimulate neurons, cells that trigger the brain's reward system, which releases dopamine, a 'neurotransmitter that plays a key role in the brain's reward centers, and can lead to pleasure producing behavior, such as drug abuse and overeating.'[31]

Howard Moskowitz, a marketing expert and experimental psychologist, coined the term 'bliss point' to identify the natural amount of sweetness, saltiness and fattiness that makes foods and beverages most enjoyable.[32] Chemists micro-engineered foods with these inborn taste combinations and added colour additives and flavour compounds to create fast foods that were even more irresistible.

Dana Small from the University of Cambridge in the United Kingdom has argued that food addiction, such as binge eating and other compulsive behaviours, does exist, although it is not as powerful as addiction to addictive drugs.[33] Existing research, including both animal and human studies, offers a number of findings that suggest food addictions. There are striking similarities between the brain patterns of people consuming excess amounts of sugar and those of heroin or cocaine users. These relationships suggest that certain foods and well-known addictive substances compete for the same brain pathways, which would help to explain why people who quit smoking may turn to food as a substitute for cigarettes.[34]

Scientific evidence also suggests that fatty, salty and sugary foods can trigger addictive behaviours. Recently researchers have gone further, stating that some people who overeat do have an addiction. Discussing a study on the excess of sodium in kids' meals, Graham MacGregor, a professor at Queen Mary University, London, concluded, 'Evidence suggests dietary habits in childhood can influence eating patterns later in life. Salt should therefore not be given to children as this could lead to a "salt addiction"', which could 'raise their blood pressure which tracks into adulthood, leading to increased risk of developing strokes and heart attacks'.[35]

Researchers now believe that food addictions contribute to the rise of obesity, and that addiction may account for the great difficulty encountered by most overweight people when they try to lose weight. In 2009 researchers at the Rudd Center for Food Policy and Obesity developed a food-addiction scale as a way to assess dependence on foods high in fat and sugar. Preliminary findings indicate that this scale can help identify people with addictive inclinations toward such foods.[36]

Healthy Options?

Fast-food chains have responded to their nutrition nightmare by offering healthier options, such as salads, but sales of such items are limited, and their inclusion on menus is often mainly for public-relations purposes. Salads and other 'healthy' items attract some adults with children to fast-food restaurants – the adults eat the salads while their children choose what they like. Fast-food companies trumpet their healthy items partly to combat the unhealthy image of their other foods and beverages. Healthy food on the menu also gives chains the ability to proclaim that eating is a 'personal responsibility', which means that companies should not be blamed if their frequent customers become ill, fat or obese.

Customers like the idea that they can order healthy food if they choose to do so, but few healthy foods have been successful. In 1991 McDonald's introduced the McLean Deluxe burger containing a 91 per cent fat-free patty with a seaweed derivative; it was dropped from the menu six years later owing to miserable sales. Salads were also introduced as healthy alternatives and were heavily promoted, but sales have been limited. In 2013 salad sales in McDonald's restaurants in the u.s. hovered between 2 and 3 per cent of total sales.[37]

There are several reasons for the minimal sales of healthy fast foods. Customers identify fast-food items marketed as healthy, lean or low-calorie as flavourless. For many customers, eating out is a treat, and they want food that tastes good – that is, high-calorie foods filled with plenty of salt, fat and sugar. Also, healthy items cost more than other items. Why spend more money for healthy items that are flavourless?

While many 'healthy' options are far better nutritionally than other fast-food menu items, some turn out to be not so healthy. Fried chicken or fish sandwiches, for instance, often have as much fat and calories as extra-large burgers. McDonald's Fruit & Maple Oatmeal contains 290 calories, 4.5 grams of fat and 32 grams of sugar, more sugar than a Snickers bar. Some salads are higher in calories, fat and sodium than traditional fast-food choices such as hamburgers or tacos. When a large packet of fatty dressing – enough to drown the greens and their healthy potential – and other components, such as croutons and taco chips and shells, are added, some fast-food salads weigh in with as much as 1,300 calories, 54 grams of fat and 1,700 milligrams of sodium.

Labelling

Despite these well-publicized claims of improved nutritional content, the amount of salt, fat and calories remains high in fast food, and publicly touted positive changes have made little overall difference, according to a study at Tufts University published in 2014. It compared the nutritional content of eighteen fast-food menu offerings in 1996 with the same items in 2013: six contained fewer calories, but nine contained more. Similarly the sodium content was lower in five of the eighteen items, but higher in seven.[38]

While most fast-food companies list the nutritional content of the food and beverages they sell on their websites, many health activists have advocated requiring chains to post calorie content in their stores. The assumption is that when customers know the calorie and nutritional content, they will make more rational decisions about the food they eat and have a better chance of avoiding chronic diseases associated with weight gain. New York and other cities have mandated nutritional labelling in chain restaurants. In the u.s. the Patient Protection and Affordable Care Act, passed in 2010, requires chain restaurants to post nutritional information in plain sight in their stores.

The effectiveness of menu labelling in reducing calorie consumption at fast-food restaurants has been questioned. A University of Washington study published in 2010 found that when parents were provided with calorie information, they chose meals containing around 100 fewer calories for their three- to six-year-old children than parents who didn't have that information. Other studies have found that menu labelling had no impact on calorie consumption in outlets. TacoTime, a Mexican American-themed fast-food restaurant chain, placed nutritional information (calories, fat and sodium) at all its 350 outlets. One study published found that menu labelling at TacoTime did not promote healthier food-purchasing behaviour. Another study concluded that calorie counts made little difference in the choices low-income people made in KFC, McDonald's, Burger King and Wendy's restaurants in New York and

New Jersey. Brian Elbel, the lead researcher in the study, concluded that 'labeling is not likely to be enough to influence obesity in a large scale way. Other public policy approaches, as well as the efforts of food companies and other actors, will be needed.'[39]

In January 2005 Ireland required that fast-food wrappers carry the message 'Fast food should be eaten in moderation as part of a balanced diet.'[40] An Australian, Aaron Schultz, the founder of the Game Changer movement, has proposed that nutritional information be posted directly on each paper wrapper, box and cup, and that it be accompanied by obesity warnings, similar to the cancer warnings on cigarette packs.[41]

4
MARKETING

In 1960 John Gibson and Oscar Goldstein acquired the McDonald's franchise for the Washington, DC, area. To gain visibility for their fast-food outlets, Gibson and Goldstein sponsored a children's television programme called 'Bozo's Circus'. Like McDonald's itself, the programme was franchised – licensed to be produced locally in different markets with their own cast, crew, and sponsors. For the local DC programme, the actor Willard Scott (later to become the jocular weatherman on *The Today Show*) played Bozo. Part of his job was to cajole young viewers into asking their parents to take them to McDonald's.

After his three-year run on the show ended, a clown-costumed Scott appeared for Gibson and Goldstein at the grand openings of their new McDonald's outlets. As the three debated what to name their reinvented 'Bozo', an ad agency proposed 'Archie McDonald', an allusion to McDonald's Golden Arches symbol. But there was a sportscaster in the DC area named Arch McDonald, so that wouldn't do. Using a simple rhyme, Scott came up with 'Ronald McDonald', and beginning in October 1963, portrayed him in the first commercials produced by a local McDonald's franchisee. Sales in Washington, DC, grew by a whopping 30 per cent per year.

In 1965, the year of the company's first public stock offering, McDonald's sponsored the broadcast of Macy's Thanksgiving Day Parade in New York City – a nationally televised event. Ronald McDonald was featured, but he was played by Coco, a clown from the Barnum & Bailey Circus; management had judged Willard Scott too fat to play the part. No fast-food chain had ever advertised on national television, and it was a financial risk because the busy season for McDonald's was the summer; but this promotion boosted McDonald's national sales by 22 per cent.

The reason for this tremendous success was clear: Ronald McDonald appealed to children, who had not previously been considered important customers for fast food. The immediate nationwide response to the Thanksgiving Day commercials paved the way for McDonald's to spend more on TV advertising, giving the chain an edge in the children's market.

The character 'Ronald McDonald' became McDonald's official spokesman in 1966 and appeared in a McDonald's commercial during the very first Super Bowl, in January 1967. When McDonald's signed a contract to open 300 outlets at military bases, Ronald McDonald posed for pictures in front of an aircraft carrier. The first Ronald McDonald House – a residence adjacent to a hospital, providing free or inexpensive room and board for families with children who required extended hospital care – was set up at the St Christopher's Hospital for Children in Philadelphia in 1974. Since then, 200 more have been constructed in the United States and eleven in other countries. All are sponsored by local McDonald's operations. In 1984 Ronald McDonald House Charities was founded in honour of Ray Kroc. Today it is one of the largest organizations financially devoted to the welfare of children and has provided housing and meals for the families of more than 2 million seriously ill children.

On a smaller scale, Ronald McDonald's image has been emblazoned on child-orientated promotional products such as book covers, colouring books, comic books, dolls, masks, Frisbees, calendars, mugs, napkins, postcards, puppets, records, drinking glasses and toy trains and trucks. The millions of dollars spent on child-orientated television advertising and local promotions have paid off: in 1980 a survey reported that 96 per cent of American children recognized Ronald McDonald (only Santa Claus got a higher rating). Today Ronald is one of the most-recognized characters for children the world over.

Other chains have followed the lead of McDonald's in targeting their advertising at children and teenagers. Fast-food advertising has certainly done its work; or, as critics might say, taken its toll. One survey, performed between 2003 and 2008, showed that 33 per cent of American children and 41 per cent of teenagers consumed fast food every day.[1] The Rudd Center research project found that in 2012, the fast-food industry spent $4.6 billion to promote 'mostly unhealthy' products, and children and teens remained the key audience for that advertising.[2]

Background

Youngsters have little buying power, but they do have the nag factor or pester power at their disposal. Research indicates that requests from children spurred about one-third of family trips to fast-food restaurants. Kids love fast food because it's a 'fun' break from traditional meals at home. It is also mainly finger food – no need to wield forks or knives, and no nagging from adults about table manners. From the fast-food industry's perspective, children are the ideal target. They are more susceptible to manipulation, and targeting them produces long-term benefits: childhood experiences shape adult habits. Children form strong bonds with brands – attachments that can last a lifetime.[3] For 50 years fast-food chains have directed the majority of their marketing at children and adolescents. As Sriram Madhusoodanan, a spokesperson for Corporate Accountability International, has explained, the fast-food industry employs 'the same cradle-to-grave marketing strategy that tobacco used: Hook them early and hook them for life.'[4]

By the time American children are three years old, they recognize an average of 100 brand logos, many of which are for fast-food chains. There are good reasons for this recognition: for starters, the major proportion of advertisements on children's television programmes are for fast-food chains. Over the last 50 years chains have developed a variety of techniques to entice children: playgrounds in fast-food outlets, cartoon characters, kids' meals and toys, television advertising and movie tie-ins. During the past two decades advertising budgets, along with the number of ads targeting children, have dramatically increased in many countries. This is largely because of the expansion of commercial cable television channels and a rise in the number of television programmes targeting children, as well as the Internet and smartphone apps.

Playgrounds

Once Ronald McDonald proved that child-centric advertising was the way to go, Ray Kroc set about remaking McDonald's outlets into exciting places for children. The McDonald's in Chula Vista, California, near San Diego, opened the first McDonaldland Park in 1972. Ten thousand people visited during its two-day grand opening. Soon the chain began opening 'McDonald's Playlands' at many outlets. Indoors or outside, these featured brightly coloured climbing structures, swings and slides, and statues of characters like Mayor McCheese and the Hamburglar. Eventually about 40 per cent of the American McDonald's outlets had PlayPlaces, and the company is now the largest private operator of playgrounds in the world. Following their lead, Burger King and other chains installed play areas at their restaurants.

Today, however, the number of playgrounds is declining – and for good reason. Children have been injured while playing and lawsuits have ensued. Playgrounds have also come under scrutiny for their poor sanitation standards. In 2011 Erin M. Carr-Jordan, a child development professor, swabbed the equipment in fast-food playgrounds in seven different states. When lab-tested for microbes, only one sample came back without pathogens. Other tests found high levels of pathogens, including foecal coliform bacteria, *Staphylococcus aureus, E. coli enteritis, Shigella, Campylobacter enteritis* and even cholera – to name a few. Analysts have concluded that playground equipment in many fast-food establishments was not being cleaned properly – sometimes not at all.

Kids' Meals

Children can burn calories playing on swings and slides, but they would have to put in a lot of playtime to counteract the excess calories they get from fast food. A World Health Organization report of 2015 concluded that the marketing of energy-dense foods and fast foods was a 'probable' cause of increasing weight gain and obesity among the world's children.[5] One obvious reason for this is that fast-food chains target children in their marketing, as the previous chapter documents. According to the McDonald's nutrition website, Happy Meal calorie counts range from 380 to 580 and sodium levels from 460 mg to 710 mg. But these figures are based on orders of small fries and 1 per cent low-fat milk. Most kids opted for larger orders of fries and sugary sodas. In 2010, researchers at the Rudd Center for Food Policy and Obesity at Yale analysed 3,039 possible kids' meal combinations from fast-food restaurants and found that only twelve theoretical meals met standards for preschoolers; only fifteen met the criteria for older children.[6]

The Physicians Committee for Responsible Medicine (PCRM) revealed that some kids' meal combinations contained more than half a day's worth of calories and more than a day's recommended intake of sodium. The McDonald's Mighty Kids Meal (containing a double cheeseburger, french fries and chocolate milk) topped the list with 840 calories and 37 grams of fat. Susan Levin, the PCRM's nutrition director, stated that 'Kids shouldn't have to dodge cholesterol bombs packaged in colorful, toy-filled boxes. We're losing the war against childhood obesity, but fast-food chains are still making obscene profits by targeting children with high-fat meals.'[7]

In response to these attacks, McDonald's introduced better alternative components to their Happy Meals, such as apple slices instead of french fries, and fat-free milk rather than soda. The company also announced that every Happy Meal served in the United States and South America would include fruit. It boasted that its outlets featured yoghurt in Canada, carrot sticks in 23 countries, corn cups in thirteen markets, apple bags in Australia, salad in Israel, cherry tomatoes in Argentina, coconut water in Brazil, organic milk in the United Kingdom, pineapple spears in France, raisins in Ireland and vegetable juice in Japan.[8]

The National Restaurant Association jumped in to defend fast-food chains, claiming that the number-one food trend in fast food was the increasing number of healthful, nutritious offerings in children's meals.[9] Over the last several years, chains have downsized portions and added healthier side-dish options. But this does not necessarily mean that kids are eating healthier meals. Researchers from the Center for Science in the Public Interest (CSPI) visited 43 McDonald's outlets and found that 93 per cent of the time, kids were automatically given french fries rather than apple slices when ordering Happy Meals, and 78 per cent of the time they were first offered soft drinks rather than milk.[10] The CSPI examined the children's meals at 25 of the largest restaurant chains. Its report, 'Obesity on the Kids' Menus at Top Chains', found that 100 per cent of the children's meals offered at KFC, Sonic, Jack in the Box, Chick-fil-A and Taco Bell, and more than 90 per cent of kids' meals served at Wendy's, McDonald's, Burger King and Dairy Queen exceeded 430 calories.[11] In 2013 the CSPI found that of the possible 3,494 kids' meal combinations, 97 per cent did not meet the expert nutrition standards for children's meals.[12]

Criticism has generated some changes. In 2013 McDonald's quietly replaced soda as the default beverage in kids' meals in the United States and twenty other countries. The drinks on their children's menu are now apple juice, fat-free milk and low-fat chocolate milk. Two years later, Wendy's and Burger King did the same. Kids can still order soda on the regular menu at both chains. As many children are first exposed to soda at fast-food chains, it is hoped that these changes will decrease obesity rates in the future. But perhaps not. Fat-free milk has 12 grams of sugar (in the form of naturally occurring lactose); pure apple juice has 20 grams of sugar (naturally occurring fructose); and 1-per-cent low-fat chocolate milk has 25 grams of sugar – much of it from added high-fructose corn syrup. (The American Heart Association recommends that children limit sugar to 12–16 grams per day.) However, it is difficult for parents to insist that children drink water when they themselves are consuming high-calorie meals and sugary sodas and shakes.

Yet another change occurred in 2015 when Taco Bell announced that it would no longer sell kids' meals or give toys away with meals. But Taco Bell's annual sales of kids' meals accounted for only 0.05 per cent of its overall sales. This would be a tougher move for other chains, such as McDonald's and Burger King, that do enormous business in these meals.

Salt is yet another problem with children's meals at fast-food chains. In 2015 Consensus Action on Salt and Health, a British nonprofit, published a study of the salt content of 218 children's meals from 23 different UK eating establishments; it concluded that 28 per cent of the meals tested contained 2 grams (2,000 mg) of salt, which is more than an entire day's allowance for a child under four years old. At the top of their sodium list was the Burger King Kids Veggie Bean Burger with Small Fries, which contained 4.6 grams of salt (155 per cent of the recommended maximum intake for four- to six-year-olds). The Kids Veggie Bean Burger with Apple Fries wasn't much better, with 3.5 grams of salt.[13]

Toys

Burger Chef, a now defunct American hamburger chain, added yet another dimension to the targeting of young audiences: in 1973 it began offering the 'Funburger', a small hamburger specially designed for children that came in a colourful box with a prize inside. This led to the invention of the 'Funmeal' that bundled the burger, fries, a soda and dessert and packed them in a box with games, cartoons, punchouts and riddles. Burger Chef's success with Funmeals prompted McDonald's to launch its own child-friendly 'Happy Meals' in 1978, pairing child-size portions with a bonus toy in a colourful box. Building brand loyalty in young children became a priority at other fast-food chains, making it common to offer toys or other premiums along with kids' meals.

McDonald's marketed its Happy Meals aggressively. When the 25th anniversary of the Happy Meal rolled around,

McDonald's launched a promotion that included a Teenie Beanie Baby in its meal package. Beanie Babies – cloth animals filled with plastic pellets for a flexible, beanbag-like body – were a huge fad beginning in 1993. Customers waited in long queues for McDonald's Happy Meals with Teenie Beanie Babies inside. This campaign is considered one of the most successful promotions in the history of advertising. Before the campaign, McDonald's was selling 10 million Happy Meals per month; during the promotion, sales increased to 100 million per month. McDonald's conducted a similar promotion the following year. A research firm reported that American youngsters 'overwhelmingly chose McDonald's as their favorite fast-food restaurant'.[14]

The distribution of toys through fast-food chains has not always gone smoothly. Millions of toys have been recalled because of safety issues. In 1982 McDonald's recalled nearly 10 million Playmobil toys because they represented a potential choking hazard. Ten years later, McDonald's recalled its 'Doc DeLorean Car' for the same reason. In 1999, 25 million of Burger King's Pokémon toys were recalled after several kids got parts caught in their throats and two suffocated to death. In 2010 McDonald's recalled 12 million Shrek-themed drinking glasses, which contained cadmium. In 2014 McDonald's recalled 2.3 million Hello Kitty-themed whistles owing to a potential choking hazard.[15]

Despite such setbacks, *Advertising Age* reported in 2010 that the advertising of Happy Meals accounted for 8 to 10 per cent of all measured-media spending in the United States, and 87 per cent of six- and seven-year-olds and 80 per cent of eight- and nine-year-olds said they 'enjoyed getting a toy with their kids' meals'. Annual sales of Happy Meals generated about $3 billion for McDonald's, which is roughly equal to the total annual sales revenue of Panera Bread or Dairy Queen.[16] In 2006 the Federal Trade Commission reported that the fast-food industry spent more than $360 million on toys to help sell more than 1 billion meals to kids under the age of twelve. These toy giveaways were the industry's second-highest youth expenditure after television advertising ($583 million).[17] A 2013 study found that 69 per cent of fast-food ads aimed at children mentioned toy giveaways.[18] At 1.5 billion toys annually, McDonald's is the world's largest toy distributor.[19]

As concern has grown about childhood obesity, critics have focused attention on the lure of the fast-food toy.[20] In 2010 Santa Clara, California, passed an ordinance setting standards for restaurant toy giveaways. In November of the same year San Francisco's city supervisors voted to ban the inclusion of toys in fast-food meals unless the meals contained fewer than 600 calories, included vegetables and fruit, and met other nutritional standards. San Francisco's mayor vetoed the bill, claiming that 'Doing these types of toy bans is inappropriate, I don't think particularly effective, and I just think it goes way too far in inserting government to try to be the decision-maker in someone's life as opposed to parents.'[21] The city supervisors thought otherwise and overrode the mayor's veto.

San Francisco followed Santa Clara's lead when it required that meals offering a free toy with purchase meet strict nutri-tional standards. Other American cities are also considering banning toys in children's fast-food meals. (McDonald's dodged this rule by charging 10 cents extra and continuing to distribute toys with Happy Meals.) The government of Chile passed a similar law in June 2012, requiring fast-food restaurants to eliminate the practice of including free toys in their packages.[22] Australia KFC has announced that they will be removing toys from their meals.[23] Procon, Brazil's consumer protection agency, fined McDonald's $1.6 million for targeting children with its child-centric advertising and Happy Meal toys.[24] Burger King New Zealand stopped giving away toys with its kids' meals in 2014,[25] but other fast-food chains have yet to follow their lead.

In 2010 the CSPI filed a class-action suit against McDonald's on behalf of Monet Parham, a mother of two from Sacramento, California. The CSPI claimed that the toys in Happy Meals represented a 'creepy and predatory' ploy that undermined the efforts of parents to encourage a healthy diet. The toys were used as 'bait' to lure children into gorging on 'unhealthy junk food'. The lawsuit claimed that 'Children eight and younger do not have the cognitive skills and the developmental maturity to understand the persuasive intent of marketing and advertising.' Michael Jacobson, the executive director of the CSPI, claimed that 'multi-billion-dollar corporations make parents' job nearly impossible by giving away toys and bombarding kids with slick advertising.'[26]

The lawsuit was dismissed in 2012 by a Superior Court judge who concluded that legally McDonald's had done nothing wrong. But the judge made no determination as to whether McDonald's did anything ethically wrong in its massive 50-year advertising campaign targeting children and promoting sugary, salty, fattening foods and beverages.

Schools and Hospitals

For years American fast-food chains have targeted public schools with the most insidious kinds of advertising. McDonald's and other chains have sponsored sports teams, gym classes, and other school programmes. A 2000 survey found that 24 per cent of districts in California had fast-food or beverage contracts giving those companies exclusive advertising rights, including displaying signs promoting their products on buses, in hallways and at sporting venues, and the placement of the company's name and logo on school equipment and facilities, such as scoreboards, bulletin boards, rooftops and even curricular materials, including textbooks and their covers.[27]

Fast-food companies have even produced educational materials on which their brand names – and often their products – are prominently displayed. Almost two-thirds of elementary schools provide money-saving coupons as student incentives.[28] Other companies developed academic contests, such as Pizza Hut's 'Book It!' programme, in which students achieving reading targets are rewarded with a certificate for a Personal Pan Pizza. The Sonic hamburger chain's 'Limeades for Learning' solicits educators for potential projects and funds up to $600 for those who receive the largest number of votes.[29] Many fast-food chains offer free or reduced-cost breakfasts to students on particular days. Other chains run fundraisers for which the schools sell fast-food coupon books to students and their families, and keep a percentage of the gross.

McDonald's spends millions of dollars annually distributing sophisticated educational programmes, with videos featuring sports figures encouraging children to be active. Domino's 'Encounter Math' ('Count on Domino's') materials are highly commercial, with activities involving pizza labelled as Domino's, the company's logo on all materials, and its name mentioned in the text. Dunkin' Donuts' programme 'Grade A Donuts: Honoring Homework Stars' offered doughnuts to those who successfully completed their homework. But critics object that greasy, sugary doughnuts – or half-price burgers or sweetened soft drinks – should not be the reward for completing homework, reading books or engaging in sports.

Some materials given to teachers for use in classrooms include nutritional information, but none discuss the high levels of sugar, salt, fat, saturated fat or calories in fast food. These teaching materials are intended to show that these companies are interested in health and education. But they neglect to mention that consuming fast food contributes to ill-health. Such promotional materials are intended to deflect attention from legitimate concerns about the nutritional quality of fast food. By providing materials free of charge, fast-food chains undercut the distribution of nonpartisan material on nutrition that is provided by medical and governmental groups.

Still more fast-food advertising was conveyed through Channel One, a digital provider owned by Houghton Mifflin Harcourt, which is viewed by an estimated 5 million students in American upper elementary and secondary schools every day. It originally broadcast ten minutes of news and two minutes of advertisements. Fast-food chains advertised on Channel One, and surveys showed that students viewing the programming had more positive attitudes towards the advertised products and were more likely to report intentions to purchase them, compared to students who did not have Channel One in their classrooms.[30] Bowing to public pressure, fast-food companies removed their advertisements from Channel One.

Chains have partnered with local schools on branded educational events and fundraisers. On 'McTeacher's Nights' or 'McStaff Nights', school staff work at a local McDonald's for a few hours, and a portion of the sales made during that shift goes to support their school.[31] In Texas students work (unpaid) for a week during the summer. The programmes, called Camp Mickey D's, are held at local McDonald's outlets and are intended to help students better understand the demands of the workplace. Others have called it free labour.

Some school cafeterias also serve brand-name fast foods. McDonald's, Taco Bell, Panda Express, Little Caesar's, Pizza Hut, Chick-fil-A, Subway and Quiznos all sell their brand-name burgers, sandwiches, pizza and chicken directly to students in American high-school cafeterias.[32] Branded fast food is available at least once a week at 10 per cent of American elementary schools, 18 per cent of middle schools and 30 per cent of high schools, while 19 per cent of high schools serve these foods daily.[33] Schools permit these commercial relationships because sponsorship generates money for school programmes that are not covered by local tax dollars.

Yet another way that fast-food chains prey on kids and teens is by locating outlets near schools. A 2005 study of fast-food outlets in Chicago found that 78 per cent of the city's schools had at least one within easy walking distance, and that there were three to four times more fast-food restaurants within a mile of schools 'than would be expected if the restaurants were distributed throughout the city in a way unrelated to school locations'. The conclusion of those researchers was that 'Fast-food restaurants are concentrated within a short walking distance from schools, exposing children to poor-quality food environments in their school neighborhoods.'[34]

Other studies support these findings. A systematic review of three million students in 2010 concluded that the presence of a fast-food restaurant within one-tenth of a mile of a school was 'associated with at least a 5.2 percent increase in the obesity rate in that school'. Proximity to fast food increased calorie intake by 30 to 100 calories per school day.[35] In New York City a preliminary investigation found that schools in neighbourhoods with the highest obesity rates had 18–28 fast-food outlets within a tenth of a mile (160 metres).[36] A 2011 study concluded that fast-food restaurants were clustered near high schools with higher obesity rates. The researchers also found that many students who patronized these outlets consumed from 30 per cent to 75 per cent of the total daily recommended allowance of calories in a single after-school snack.[37] Yet another study found that students who have fast-food restaurants near their schools eat fewer fruits and vegetables and drink more soda. They were more 'likely to be overweight than were youths whose schools were not near fast-food restaurants, after we controlled for student- and school-level characteristics'. The researchers surmised that adolescent obesity could be reduced if fast-food chains were not permitted near schools.[38]

Daily consumption of fast food not only contributes to obesity, but may hurt academic performance. Students who consumed high levels of fast food in the fifth grade scored lower three years later on maths, reading and science tests compared with students who ate no fast food.[39]

While the connection between schools and fast food is particularly problematic in the u.s., companies have at least proposed relationships with schools in other countries as well. In the UK McDonald's distributes teaching aids and offers school presentations on work-related learning.[40] In Australia a McDonald's outlet proposed to deliver burgers, fries, nuggets and desserts to schools for lunch and special occasions. In return the schools were to receive cash rebates and free drinks. Jane Martin, the Executive Manager of the Obesity Policy Committee in Victoria, Australia, responded: 'This deliberate targeting of children in these settings shows that McDonald's is putting profit ahead of children's health. This is from a company that claims to be committed to "responsible" advertising to children.'[41]

In addition to schools, fast-food chains have also opened outlets in hospitals. At least 59 of America's 250 paediatric hospitals offered fast food, reported a study in 2005.[42] McDonald's, Wendy's and Chick-fil-A had contracts in hospitals not just to serve workers and guests but patients as well. Hospitals in the UK also sell fast food. In 2013 a cardiologist at the Royal Free Hospital in London criticized these arrangements in an article published in the *British Medical Journal*.[43] McDonald's, Burger King, Costa Coffee and Greggs (a bakery chain) operated outlets in 100 hospitals, including Guy's in London and Addenbrooke's in Cambridge.

In March 2015 a committee in Parliament finally got round to demanding that the National Health Service close all fast-food operations in hospitals.[44]

Movie Tie-ins

Cross-promotion advertising campaigns have connected fast-food chains and films since the mid-1970s. When George Lucas's Lucasfilm released its blockbuster *Star Wars* in 1977, it partnered with Burger Chef, which gave away a poster starring C-3PO, R2-D2 and other characters from the movie; Burger King sold a set of drinking glasses featuring the film's main characters. But it wasn't until the 1990s that the fast-food industry really began to take advantage of movie tie-ins. These promotional campaigns typically include on-screen exterior shots of fast-food chains; posters; advertisements on cups, bags and containers; toys representing characters from the movie; and competitions offering tickets to showings or other special events. The toys and other merchandise are given away with a purchase, or sometimes sold outright at a modest price. The chains still make a substantial profit on the sale of these items, which naturally account for a lot of food sales.

Fast-food chains have a particular interest in films made for children. In 1994 Burger King and the Walt Disney Company signed a ten-film promotional contract that included *Aladdin* (1992), *Beauty and the Beast* (1991), *The Lion King* (1994) and *Toy Story* (1995). In 1999 Burger King formed a partnership with the Pokémon franchise (a Japanese video game that spawned many offshoots). In 2005

Burger King bought into Lucasfilm and Twentieth Century Fox's *Star Wars: Episode III – Revenge of the Sith* and *The Fantastic Four,* and the burger chain recently signed an agreement with Marvel Enterprises, Inc. (formerly Marvel Comics), a subsidiary of the Walt Disney Company, to distribute Marvel-related merchandise including toys based on Marvel's 'Super Hero Squad' and on Marvel movies, such as *Thor* and *Captain America: The First Avenger.*

In 1996 the Walt Disney Company agreed to a ten-year global marketing agreement with McDonald's Corporation. McDonald's promoted Disney's films; in return McDonald's placed Disney toys in its Happy Meals and sold spin-off products, such as lunchboxes. In 1997 McDonald's made a deal for a tie-in with Disney's movie *Flubber.* The movie was not a great hit but the tie-in was considered a success. In 2005 McDonald's tied in with Disney's *Herbie: Fully Loaded* and Miramax's *The Adventures of Shark Boy and Lava Girl.* Wendy's went in with Warner Bros.' *Charlie and the Chocolate Factory.* In 2006 McDonald's Happy Meals and Mighty Kids' Meals came with toys based on characters from the Walt Disney Pictures/ Walden Media film *The Chronicles of Narnia: The Lion, the Witch and the Wardrobe.* But in 2006 Disney discontinued its marketing relationship with McDonald's, citing concerns about the healthfulness of fast food, particularly its contribution to childhood obesity.

McDonald's used a tie-in with *Shrek the Third*, which premiered in 2007, to promote two of its more healthful children's options: sliced apples and low-fat milk. Shrek's image appeared on Happy Meal milk jugs and bags of Apple Dippers (which come with caramel sauce). McDonald's has also released games starring Shrek, such as 'Shrek Forever After', in which Shrek encourages kids to 'Shrek Out' their Happy Meals with healthy menu options. More recent McDonald's tie-ins include *Avatar*, *Night at the Museum: Battle of the Smithsonian* and *Ice Age: Dawn of the Dinosaurs*. Hardee's and Carl's Jr. promoted their Super Bacon Cheeseburger through their tie-in with the movie *Man of Steel* in 2013.

Chains have introduced menu items inspired by movies. When *Star Wars: Episode 1* was released in 1999, the French fast-food chain Quick introduced the 'Dark Vador' Burger, Jedi Burger and Dark Burger at their restaurants. Burger King introduced the triple Whopper with cheese ('to satisfy even Kong-sized cravings') and a 46-ounce (1.36 litre) chocolate-banana milkshake when the remake of *King Kong* was released in 2005. The Subway sandwich chain was featured in 2009's *Land of the Lost*, and one of the movie's reptilian characters appeared in a Subway commercial; the chain also commissioned an online *Land of the Lost* game as a tie-in. McDonald's in Hong Kong offered Batman's 'Diner Double Beef' (the connection between this creation and the movie is not obvious). When *Twilight: New Moon* was released in 2009, Burger King sold *Twilight*-themed hamburgers. When the 2010 movie *Captain America* came out, Baskin-Robbins sold Hydra-Force Sundaes, Super Soldier Sundaes and Captain America Ice Cream Cake. Two years later it introduced Lunar Cheesecake ice cream as a tie-in with the movie *Men in Black 3*. The green ice cream was based on a recipe originally devised in 1969 to celebrate the NASA moon landing. In 2015 Dairy Queen partnered with

Universal Pictures to create the Jurassic Smash Blizzard in conjunction with the release of *Jurassic World*.

These are just a few of the hundreds of fast-food movie tie-ins. They have generated millions of dollars from box office attendance and the sale of toys and other merchandise, as well as food sales. Movie tie-ins are present in 55 per cent of children's advertisements on television.[45]

Television Advertising

American children spend an average of three hours a day watching television, so this medium significantly shapes their buying habits. In 1983 the Federal Trade Commission (FTC) lifted many regulations pertaining to advertisements aired during children's television programmes. Into this gap leapt the fast-food chains, saturating kids' television with commercials. The Happy Meal has long been a heavily marketed item. According to *Advertising Age*, in 2010 McDonald's promotion for the Happy Meal accounted for 8 to 10 per cent of all measured-media spending in the United States.[46]

The Children's Television Act, enacted by the FTC in 1990, limited air time for commercials during children's programming to 12 minutes per hour on weekdays and 10.5 minutes per hour at weekends.[47] Still, during the past twenty years there has been a dramatic increase in the number of commercials aired and the money spent on advertising. This is largely caused by the expansion of commercial cable television channels and the increase in the number of programmes targeting children.

Many studies have offered evidence that children's TV advertising is indeed effective at persuading children to want the product advertised. Children pay attention to commercials because they like the 'messengers' – usually cartoon characters. Company 'spokescharacters', such as Ronald McDonald, create favourable attitudes towards specific brands. This is a particularly effective technique for young children, who can recognize characters by two to three years of age but do not have the capacity to understand the persuasive intent behind the advertisement.

Making television commercials even more powerful is the fact that many children aged between two and eighteen have a television in their bedrooms. This means that youngsters are increasingly experiencing advertising without any parental supervision or mediation.[48] Researchers have found a relationship between the amount of time children spend watching television and their weight: in short, children who watch more, weigh more. A sedentary lifestyle is one reason frequent TV-watchers gain weight, but another is fast-food advertising. A report issued by the Institute of Medicine of the National Academies in 2006 found compelling evidence linking food advertising on television with increased childhood obesity, and early TV habits may have long-lasting effects: two studies that followed children from birth found that TV viewing in childhood predicts obesity risk well into adulthood and mid-life.[49]

Some fast-food companies have agreed voluntarily to cut back on their television advertising. In 2006 the Children's Food and Beverage Advertising Initiative (CFBAI), a voluntary corporate self-regulation programme, was launched.

Members pledged to reduce the use of third-party licensed characters in advertising primarily directed to children; not seek food and beverage product placement in editorial or entertainment content that is primarily directed to children; revise interactive games that are primarily directed to children that promote the company's food or beverages; and, finally, stop all advertisement of food or beverages in elementary schools.[50]

Despite the voluntary agreement, between 2003 and 2007 fast-food advertising on children's television in America increased by more than 20 per cent for programmes aimed at children between the ages of twelve and seventeen; more than 12 per cent for ages six to eleven; and nearly 5 per cent for ages two to five. Researchers at Yale University's Rudd Center for Food Policy and Obesity looked at data from the Nielsen Company assessing trends in television food advertising among children and adolescents; they concluded that preschoolers saw 56 per cent more ads for Subway, 21 per cent more ads for McDonald's and 9 per cent more ads for Burger King in 2009 than they had done two years before.[51] In 2013 the Federal Trade Commission reported that fast-food companies spent $714 million on television ads marketing directly to young people aged between two and seventeen.[52] A 2014 study examined the television advertising of Burger King and McDonald's (both CFBAI members) and concluded that the fast-food industry's self-regulation 'failed to achieve a de-emphasis on toy premiums and tie-ins and did not adequately communicate healthy menu choices'.[53]

In 2012 the National Bureau of Economic Research, one of America's leading research organizations, examined comprehensive data on the viewing habits, health and lifestyles of 13,000 American children. The study concluded that banning fast-food advertising on children's television would reduce obesity levels in children between the ages of eight and eleven by 18 per cent, and in children aged twelve to eighteen by 14 per cent.[54]

Other countries are far ahead of the U.S. in restricting fast-food advertising on television. Sweden, Norway, Greece, Finland, Denmark, Ireland, the UK, Belgium and Malaysia have banned or restricted such ads on children's television programmes, and other countries are considering similar bans. Studies show, however, that many fast-food ads are seen by children who watch adult programming during the 8–9 pm time slot. In 2015, when in opposition, the Labour Party in the UK announced proposals to ban television advertisements for fast food (as well as alcohol, cigarettes and junk food) before 9 pm. (It also proposed a cap on the amount of sugar, salt and fat in children's food products.) In New Zealand both Burger King and McDonald's have stopped running television ads for their kids' meals.[55]

Online, Mobile and Viral Marketing

Fast-food chains have created voluntary codes to regulate television ads aimed at children, but the companies do not apply the same restrictions to their social media marketing and smartphone apps. During the past decade, children and adolescents have increasingly become connected through the Internet, mobile phones, smartphones, tablets and handheld music/video players. Even young children now have access to these new technologies: 80 per cent of children under the age of five use the Internet weekly, and 60 per cent of those aged three and younger watch online videos. This has created an unprecedented opportunity for advertisers to connect directly with children and teenagers who are usually not under adult supervision when they are online or on the phone.

Fast-food companies have extensive programmes to reach youngsters through these technologies. This includes marketing that encourages children to visit corporate websites, such as Burger King's BKCrown. com and McDonald's HappyMeal.com. One website, www.ronald.com, specifically targets preschoolers. The KFC Fun Crew! only allows kids aged between three and twelve to join.[56] According to the Pew Report *Social Media and Mobile Internet Use Among Teens and Young Adults* (2010), 93 per cent of teenagers (aged twelve to seventeen) go online.[57] According to the Rudd Center, in 2009 the fast-food chain with the most monthly hits by children under the age of seventeen was Pizza Hut, followed closely by Domino's. McDonald's has more than a dozen websites for kids and teens. Other frequently visited sites are those of Burger King, KFC and Starbucks.

In addition to corporate-controlled websites, fast-food companies also place ads on youth-orientated websites. According to the Rudd Center, 71 million ads by Domino's were viewed every month on such sites. The other fast-food companies with the highest numbers of ad views are, in descending order, Pizza Hut, McDonald's, Wendy's, Burger

King, Dairy Queen, Sonic, KFC, Dunkin' Donuts, Subway, Starbucks and Taco Bell.

Fast-food chains have also begun to promote their products through viral or 'buzz' marketing, such as disseminating online videos through email. These videos are frequently shocking or funny – attention-grabbing and memorable. They usually use a soft-sell approach to promote a product or brand, and they may seem to have little to do with the product being advertised. McDonald's in China, for instance, released a video that depicted a love-struck man who finally wins over the object of his affection by offering her McDonald's coupons. It was viewed by 2.2 million people in the first week after it was released. 'Advergaming', another method of Internet marketing, is the term for online games that contain images intended to help promote products. These are particularly effective with children and adolescents. McDonald's and Burger King alone have 60 to 100 online pages of such games and 'virtual worlds' that actively engage children, according to a report released by the Rudd Center in 2010.[58] In addition to having a presence on the Internet, a number of companies, notably Starbucks and McDonald's, offer free WiFi for their customers at many of their outlets.

Fast-food chains have been particularly active in social media. They engage their customers with promotions for their latest menu offerings, and social media permit feedback from customers. Many chains send their fans e-coupons that can be redeemed for discounts. Starbucks has frequently been identified as a fast-food company with successful online media, followed by McDonald's, Panera

Bread, Subway and Dunkin' Donuts. In 2015 Engagement Labs, a technology and data company, identified Pizza Hut and Wendy's as the most successful American fast-food companies on Facebook and Twitter.[59]

An unusual social media campaign targeting sixteen- to 26-year-olds was launched by KFC in China in December 2014. It featured a Korean-themed combo meal that included a figurine of a highly popular band, called EXO, which has South Korean and Chinese members. The figurine had a QR barcode on the bottom. Customers with smartphones could use the code to download an app with a dancing game set to the band's music.[60] Starbucks is the current American leader in mobile/digital engagement. Its smartphone app permits customers to order, pay and tip baristas using their phones. In 2013 about 90 per cent of total store spending ($1.6 billion) was accomplished with smartphones.[61]

Perhaps the most tasteless social media campaign to date was conceived and executed by Burger King Russia. In 2015 the company paid about $10 for a promotional 'Tittygram' with the words 'I love Burger King' in Russian lettered in red on a well-endowed woman's chest. They posted it on their official company site on VK.com (the Russian equivalent of Facebook). Burger King Russia's sales may or may not have gone up, but the 'Tittygram' went viral on the Internet, immediately received huge visibility and attracted widespread condemnation.[62]

Fast-food companies also advertise or promote themselves directly or indirectly on YouTube. Chipotle Mexican Grill, a fast-casual chain, claims that its foods are grown and raised without pesticides, antibiotics or hormones, and are not produced on factory farms. It has used the fear of factory farming to promote its foods: its YouTube animated video *The Scarecrow* has been seen by more than 14 million viewers since it was released in 2013. It is the companion piece to a Chipotle mobile app-based game for iPhone and iPad.[63]

In addition to advertising, companies pay young people to promote their products through social media, where they engage in viral and buzz marketing. As children and adolescents increasingly acquire mobile phones and other portable electronics and pick up on new applications, companies keep pace, determined to stay in touch with the youth market. Advertisers have developed programmes to reach their target audience directly via texting and other forms of messaging. On 5 March 2012 Domino's UK announced on Twitter that they would reduce the price of pizza on that day according to how many people tweeted about the promotion in time for lunch. Thanks to the large number of tweets, the pizza price for that day dropped from £15.99 to £7.74.

Fast-food chains also use social networking sites such as Twitter and Facebook for timely responses to public relations problems. Taco Bell responded via social media when a 2011 lawsuit claimed that the company engaged in false advertising by stating that the meat in its tacos was 'seasoned beef', when in fact the taco filling contained only 35 per cent beef. Taco Bell responded with a major campaign on Facebook that offered a free 'crunchy seasoned beef taco' and the controversy quietly faded away.

Viral marketing campaigns are difficult to generate, but several fast-food promotional efforts have succeeded. In 1999 Pizza Hut placed their logo on an unmanned rocket that supplied the International Space Station. A year later it delivered pizza to the station.[64] In 2004, on its branded interactive website, Burger King introduced the 'Subservient Chicken' – a person dressed in a chicken costume who would perform selected acts as directed by the viewer. The site had more than 100 million hits in the two weeks after its launch. Ten years later, Burger King brought back the 'Subservient Chicken' to promote a new menu item.[65] In 2007 the company posted 'The Whopper Freakout', a video presenting customers' reactions to a notice stating that Burger King's premier product, the Whopper, would no longer be available. The company integrated this website with its television advertising.

In February 2015 McDonald's Italy released a twenty-second YouTube video showing a pizzeria waiter asking a young boy what kind of pizza he would like. The boy responds, 'A Happy Meal.' The next scene shows the family with a now happy boy with his Happy Meal in McDonald's.[66] The video was so successful that the True Neapolitan Pizza Association (Associazione Verace Pizza Napoletana) threatened to sue McDonald's for 'pizza defamation', calling the video's premise – that Italian children preferred Happy Meals to pizza – 'blasphemy'.[67] Of course, such complaints generated greater visibility for the video. Within a month it had been watched by more than 100,000 people. Due to criticism, however, the company removed the video from YouTube.

Viral campaigns have also harmed fast-food chains. In 2012 McDonald's used the hashtag #McDStories to encourage Twitter users to share fond memories of experiences with the chain. Twitter users responded with everything from light sarcasm to savage criticism, changing the hashtag into a '#bashtag'.[68] A video of a Taco Bell employee licking a stack of empty taco shells went viral in 2013 when it was posted on the Taco Bell Facebook page (and subsequently removed). The company claimed that the shells were thrown out and not served to customers. It also fired the employee.[69] Around the same time, a photograph of a Wendy's employee slurping soft-serve ice cream directly from the dispenser nozzle was posted on Reddit, a social networking site, and promptly it too went viral.

Iconic Opposition

McDonald's is the largest fast-food chain in the world based on sales. Its mascot, Ronald McDonald, is not just an advertising gimmick – he has become a symbol of the entire fast-food industry. As a result, he has been a target for critics and protesters who are upset with the policies and products of McDonald's and of fast-food culture in general. In 2000 Hong Kong protesters dressed as Ronald McDonald carried signs stating that the company was exploiting workers in China – referring to the alleged use of child labour by McDonald's suppliers. Corporate Accountability International (CAI) has launched a campaign to retire Ronald McDonald. The organization believes that as a promotional tool for McDonald's, he contributes to childhood obesity. CAI is opposed to all fast-food advertising that targets children. It has set up a website for young people called 'Retire Ronald' and in May 2010 issued a report, *Clowning with Kids' Health: The Case for Ronald McDonald's Retirement.*

The McDonald's Corporation responded by proclaiming that Ronald McDonald is 'the heart and soul of Ronald McDonald House Charities, which lends a helping hand to families in their time of need, particularly when families need to be near their critically-ill children in hospitals'. Another response to these attacks has been the company's attempts to give Ronald McDonald a healthier image. His website has been revamped to include games not tied to McDonald's foods or brand, and the new games involve physical activity, such as juggling and skipping. Deborah Lapidus, one of the leaders of the CAI campaign, responded that 'For nearly 50 years, Ronald McDonald has hooked kids on unhealthy foods spurring a deadly epidemic of diet-related diseases.' She added, 'Ronald deserves a break and so do we.'[70]

In 2011 Finnish activists stole a statue of Ronald McDonald and produced a parody of a terrorist video threatening to harm the statue unless McDonald's answered questions, such as 'Why are you not open about the manufacturing process, raw materials and additives used in your products? What are you afraid of?' The 'kidnappers' vowed that if they did not receive an answer before their deadline, they would decapitate the statue by guillotine. Two pranksters were apprehended before the beheading could occur, and the statue was 'liberated', but other activists beheaded a replica of the statue and disseminated the video on the Internet.[71] McDonald's corporate response was that the stunt was 'in very poor taste'.

Despite the opposition to Ronald McDonald, his image can still be found in most McDonald's outlets, and he is among the most popular children's characters in the world. He speaks 25 languages, including Cantonese, Portuguese, Russian and Hindi. *Advertising Age* rated Ronald McDonald as the second most successful advertising icon of the twentieth century in the United States. (The number-one icon was the Marlboro Man, who promoted the cigarette brand.)

Reducing Advertising

Yale University's Rudd Center for Food Policy and Obesity conducted a comprehensive study of fast-food marketing and nutrition, releasing the results in 2010. The study reported that the fast-food industry spent more than $4.2 billion on marketing and advertising in 2009, focusing on television, the Internet, social media sites and mobile phone apps. Despite promises to the contrary, the fast-food industry has increased its advertising to children, and for good reason.[72] As Sriram Madhusoodanan from CAI noted, 'kids tend to interact much longer with a brand in cyberspace than they might do otherwise.'[73]

The World Health Organization has called on governments to reduce the marketing of fast food to children. Its 'Set of Recommendations on the Marketing of Foods and Non-Alcoholic Beverages to Children' called for the elimination of all advertising of such foods in nurseries, preschool centres, schools, on school grounds and playgrounds, and at family and child clinics and paediatric services.

Some countries have banned or greatly restricted all advertising on children's television. Greece forbids any television advertisements for toys before 10 pm. Child-directed advertising is significantly restricted in Denmark and Belgium. In 2001 Ireland passed legislation requiring a code for advertising that is aimed at children under eighteen years of age. It bans the use of cartoon characters and celebrities to promote food products to young audiences.[74] The Canadian Broadcasting Corporation does not accept advertising on programmes directed at children younger than twelve years. The Canadian Broadcast Code for Advertising to Children restricts the use of puppets and messages that may encourage children to buy certain products. Since 1980, the province of Quebec has prohibited advertising aimed directly at children aged thirteen years and younger on commercial television. A 2011 study concluded that as a result of the ban, fast-food sales declined by an estimated 13 per cent, and the childhood obesity rate in Quebec was significantly lower than in the rest of Canada.[75]

Sweden banned television ads targeting children younger than twelve in 1991, but the ban was challenged and in 1997 the European Court of Justice ruled that it was a restraint of trade that discriminated against foreign broadcasters. As a result of the ruling, satellite channels continue to expose Swedish children to advertising. Obesity in Sweden rose after the ban was struck down. Norway banned television ads targeting children aged twelve years and younger in 1992. In Finland advertisements that attempt to persuade children to buy products are prohibited, as are those that employ cartoon characters or child actors to market goods. Belgium prohibits ads on children's programmes and Australia has banned advertisements during TV programming for preschoolers.

In 2006 the British broadcasting regulator Ofcom announced a ban on the advertising of foods high in fat, salt and sugar on programmes aimed at children under sixteen and prohibited the use of licensed characters, celebrities and promotional offers targeting preschool or primary-school children. An assessment of this policy conducted in 2010 concluded that the ban had significantly reduced advertising seen by children.[76]

Calls for similar bans in the U.S. have repeatedly met with failure. The CSPI and Corporate Accountability International have protested against what they consider 'predatory marketing' to very young children, who are unable to differentiate commercials from regular programming. Those supporting the right of commercial companies to market their products to children claim that it is a First Amendment issue. They feel that parents should be the ones to decide what their children eat.

In 2009 the U.S. Congress created an Interagency Working Group on Food Marketed to Children, consisting of representatives of the FTC, the Food and Drug Administration, the Centers for Disease Control and the U.S. Department of Agriculture. The intention was to create voluntary nutritional guidelines for the marketing of food to children and adolescents of seventeen and younger. In July 2010 the task force gave its recommendations: foods that do not meet certain nutritional criteria, and those that exceed certain fat, sugar and sodium levels, should not be marketed to children. Specifically, advertised food must contain at least 50 per cent 'by weight of one or more of the following: fruit; vegetable; whole grain; fat-free or low-fat milk or yogurt; fish; extra lean meat or poultry; eggs; nuts and seeds; or beans'. As few fast foods meet this criteria, these recommendations, if implemented, would curtail the marketing of these products to children and adolescents.

The fast-food industry deducts the cost of advertising as a business expense. The Rudd Center estimates that the industry deducts close to $2 billion annually for the cost of producing and airing commercials on children's television programmes. Critics have urged the elimination of the tax deduction. A longitudinal study of 13,000 children over a 30-year period concluded in 2008 that banning food advertising on American television would reduce the number of overweight children aged between three and eleven in a fixed population by 18 per cent and would reduce the number of overweight adolescents aged twelve to eighteen by 14 per cent. It also concluded that eliminating the tax deductibility of such advertising would decrease overweight by 5 to 6 per cent.[77]

In low-income urban neighbourhoods residents have limited access to more expensive healthy food. Companies have actively targeted minorities in their advertising. Fast food has become overwhelmingly popular and outlets are major sources of nutrition in poor neighbourhoods. According to a report by the Rudd Center, African American children and adolescents saw 50 per cent more fast-food TV ads than white youngsters. McDonald's alone was responsible for 25 per cent of the fast-food marketing to Latino children in 2009.[78] A 2007 study reported that among Mexican American children in San Diego, four- to seven-year-olds who ate at fast-food restaurants were twice as likely to be obese as those who did not.[79] One 2015 study analysed non-media fast-food advertising, such as displays of meal toys, posters and toy images, at 6,716 fast-food restaurants and concluded that fast-food restaurants targeted children in 'majority black communities, rural areas, and middle-income communities'.[80]

In 2010 American fast-food chains spent about $580 million marketing to children under the age of twelve,[81] enabling the industry to sell about 1.2 billion kids' meals each year in the u.s. alone. They have become the standard by which children judge virtually all food.[82] Massive marketing campaigns have pushed kids toward poor eating habits and honed their cravings for salt, sugar and fat. As chains acquire a loyal, lifelong customer base, their customers may face lifelong struggles with health issues.

There is positive news, according to a study published in 2015. Based on data collected from the National Health and Nutrition Examination Surveys, the percentage of American children filling up on fast food fell from 38.8 per cent in 2003–2004 to 32.6 per cent in 2009–10. Children who did eat fast food also appear to have downsized their orders, at least in some fast-food chains.[83] Sales of kids' meals have also been declining, according to the NPD Group, a leading market research company that reported sales dropping from 1.3 billion to 1.2 billion. Ironically NPD concluded that children increasingly opted for meals from the cheaper adult 'dollar menus'.[84] American child obesity rates have declined, but it is unclear whether this is related to the decline in fast-food consumption. Whether these studies were just anomalies caused by the economic recession, or are long-lasting trends, remains to be seen.

5
ENVIRONMENT

In 1986 the London Greenpeace Group, independent activists not associated with Greenpeace International, began distributing a six-page leaflet, *What's Wrong with McDonald's? Everything They Don't Want You to Know*. The leaflet charged, among other things, that 'McDonald's and Burger King are two of the many u.s. corporations using lethal poisons to destroy vast areas of Central American rainforests to create grazing pastures for cattle to be sent back to the States as burgers and pet food, and to provide fast-food packaging materials.' It continued: 'Not only are McDonald's and many other corporations contributing to a major ecological catastrophe, they are forcing the tribal peoples in the rainforests off their ancestral territories where they have lived peacefully, without damaging their env[i]ronment, for thousands of years . . . It's no exaggeration to say that when you bite into a Big Mac, you're helping the McDonald's empire to wreck this planet.'[1]

The London Greenpeace activists distributed the flyer over a period of four years, often in front of McDonald's outlets in London. In 1990 McDonald's brought libel proceedings against the London Greenpeace activists who had distributed the pamphlet. Libel laws in the uk require defendants to prove in court the truth of their statements. Two activists, Helen Steel and Dave Morris, defended themselves. They were not given any legal help from the court, but they were assisted by the Haldane Society of Socialist Lawyers on a pro bono basis. This David-and-Goliath fight was dubbed McLibel. As news of it spread, the British media seized upon it and often the trial proceedings ended up as front-page news. The trial began in March 1994 and continued for three years, becoming the longest-running trial in British history.

It was also a major public relations disaster for McDonald's, which was required to defend itself regarding its labour, marketing, environmental, nutrition, food safety and animal welfare practices. Steel and Morris forced the company's top executives to testify for days. The McSpotlight Website covered the trial and McDonald's alleged worldwide abuses. Emails and press releases were sent out and 'Days of Action' were held around the world protesting against McDonald's actions. The original leaflet was translated into 27 different languages and, since 1990, an estimated 3 million copies have been handed out so far.

In the final judgement Morris and Steel were found to have libelled McDonald's and were fined £60,000, which they refused to pay. The judge stated that most of the Greenpeace charges of environmental degradation were unproven, but he did find that McDonald's had exploited children, endangered the health of its customers, paid workers extremely low wages and opposed union activity. He also found that the company did bear responsibility for the cruelty inflicted upon animals by many of its suppliers.

Morris and Steel appealed against the decision. On 31 March 1999 the Court of Appeal overruled parts of the original McLibel verdict, supporting the leaflet's assertion that eating McDonald's food can cause heart disease and that McDonald's employees were treated badly. The Court of Appeal reduced the damages to £40,000. In 2000 Morris and Steel filed an appeal with the European Court of Human Rights, who concluded that the defendants' right of free expression had been violated because they had not been given legal aid and therefore had been denied a fair trial. A documentary film based on the story and titled *McLibel* was released in 2005.

Background

The environmental movement that emerged in the 1970s was diverse, drawing partisans from both the mainstream and the radical fringe. Environmentalists are concerned with many different issues, such as preserving the natural beauty of the land, saving native plants and wildlife from the threat of extinction, preventing land, water and air pollution, limiting the consumption of scarce natural resources and dealing with the reality of climate change.

Global food systems have been targets for the environmental movement. Activists have advocated improved regulation and control of industrial agriculture and commercial fishing. Environmental organizations have addressed threats to health and environment, such as the use of petrochemical fertilizers, pesticides and herbicides on crops and antibiotics and hormones in animal feeding operations, waste and contaminants from food packaging, and agricultural pollution (of water, air and land). Environmentalists have developed projects to raise awareness of these issues and have lobbied for the passage of laws and regulations that would lessen agriculture's environmental impact.

Recently environmentalists have concluded that of all the choices made by consumers, few have as powerful an effect on their own health and that of the planet as what they will – and will not – eat. Food has become a platform for discussion and action on many environmental controversies. The specific environmental charges levelled at McDonald's by London Greenpeace in the McLibel case may not have been proven, but the fast-food industry is immense and it is global. Through its sheer size and its business policies, it has directly and indirectly harmed the environment through urban blight, the production of un-recyclable waste, the destruction of rainforests and the release of greenhouse gases, which have contributed to climate change.

Urban Blight

Fast-food chains have changed urban landscapes. Fast-food entrepreneurs initially focused on cities, particularly areas where large businesses were located. After the Second World War, factories and other businesses began leaving inner cities, and their employees moved out to the suburbs. The older fast-food chains, such as White Castle, with many inner-city locations, confronted a major loss of customers and a significant increase in crime and vagrancy in their neighbourhoods. Without a large working-class customer base, many locations were closed; their abandoned buildings deteriorated, contributing to neighbourhood blight.

Beginning in the 1950s, American fast-food chains turned to the highways to serve motorists. Outlets popped up on the outskirts of cities, where real estate was cheap and automobile traffic was high. Because cars sped by at a fast clip, large signs were needed to catch the driver's eye. Regardless of their size, signs were difficult to read at night, so neon lighting became common. Fast-food signs were so towering and outlandish that they alienated local residents.

Another way to attract customers was with striking architecture that made the building itself a sign – hence the creation of standardized 'logo buildings' that were instantly recognizable to potential customers. McDonald's was a leader in this, but eye-catching does not equal aesthetically pleasing: their building design met with criticism, especially for its steeply raked roof and the golden arches 'bursting' through it. Others objected to the enormous red 'handlebars' – purposeless steel brackets – on the roofs of Burger King stands. In the hope of quashing public opposition, both McDonald's and Burger King modified their designs to make them less visually disruptive.

The concerns were not limited to the design of particular chains or outlets. Commercial strips – unbroken rows of fast-food stands and other national chains along highways – were considered objectionable, too. Communities organized resistance to glaringly illuminated logo buildings. Municipalities have prevented the construction of new fast-food restaurants through zoning, while others have refused to approve new permits for such businesses.

Litter, Un-recyclable Waste and Pollution

Most fast-food chains package their meals in disposable materials – paper and plastic bags, waxed paper wrappers and cardboard boxes and cups. Because about 70 per cent of American customers leave the premises with their food, discarded burger wrappers, french-fry containers and cups frequently end up as roadside litter. Of all the rubbish found along city streets and highways, an estimated 20 per cent derives from fast-food packaging. Cities have considered charging fast-food outlets and other food distributors a litter fee based on gross sales.[2] The revenue was intended to be used to keep the city's streets, pavements and public spaces clean and sanitary.

Most fast-food chains provide single-use food and beverage packaging. Fast-food establishments, of course, place rubbish containers in convenient locations around their premises. Signs encourage customers to 'put trash in its place'. (Most chains have compactors to limit the volume of rubbish they generate, but this is a separate issue from that of the litter dropped by customers.) To counteract the damage to their reputations from piles of readily identifiable rubbish in public areas, many fast-food chains contribute to local activities, such as sponsoring highway clean-ups. However, takeaway plastic products, such as cutlery, straws and cups, can be swept into waterways and oceans, where they can harm marine life.

A related problem with fast-food litter is that the vast majority is not recycled. According to a 2012 study in Austin, Texas, 85 per cent of the waste from fast-food chains could have been recycled or composted. Chains use recycled products and recycle waste, but to date this is limited because of the lack of recycle bins, customer understanding and recycling centres, and the extra effort and costs associated with recycling, such as actually delivering it to recycling centres. Yet chains have made substantial progress on reducing waste. McDonald's Austria, for instance, recycles 95 per cent of its waste.[3]

Of all the waste generated by fast-food sales, Styrofoam (the Dow Chemical Company's brand name for its polystyrene products) has been of particular concern. Styrofoam is lightweight, strong, an excellent insulator and far cheaper than paper containers. It was widely adopted in the fast-food industry for hot food containers, such as hamburger 'clamshells' and coffee cups. In the 1990s McDonald's was the world's largest single user of polystyrene.

Styrofoam was used so extensively by the fast-food industry that it littered city streets, highways, beaches and waterways. Polystyrene has many environmental drawbacks: it cannot be economically recycled; in landfill, it eventually breaks down into small particles but does not biodegrade; if incinerated, it produces toxic emissions. Several studies identified styrene, the precursor to polystyrene, as a possible human carcinogen. Styrene, activists claimed, easily migrated from packaging into foods and beverages served in it. In 1986 the U.S. Environmental Protection Agency reported that virtually all Americans had styrene in their bodies.

On 1 August 1987 activists from an organization called 'Vermonters Organized for Clean Up' picketed a few McDonald's restaurants for their use of Styrofoam. By October 1987 the Styrofoam boycott had spread to fourteen states. The Citizens Clearinghouse for Hazardous Waste (CCHW) coordinated a nationwide 'McToxics' campaign against McDonald's to get them to stop using foam food packaging. In 1988 Suffolk County, New York (on Long Island), and the city council of Berkeley, California, banned general polystyrene foam products, including plates, cups and burger boxes. Dozens of other cities and counties around the country followed suit.

The Styrofoam issue was also raised in the McLibel trial. Paul Preston, the president of McDonald's UK, testified that if 1 million customers each bought a soft drink, he would not expect more than 100–150 cups to end up as litter. He asserted that Styrofoam packaging was less environmentally damaging than washing reusable plates, knives and forks. Despite the defence, McDonald's did eventually switch from Styrofoam clamshells to paper boxes. The chain continued to use polystyrene foam coffee cups until 2013, when it replaced them with double-walled paper cups. Other companies have yet to phase out polystyrene from their hot beverage cups and virtually all continue to use rigid polystyrene for their takeaway coffee-cup lids.

Destruction of Rainforests

The London Greenpeace group and other organizations have charged fast-food chains with contributing to the destruction of the rainforests. Some chains do buy products, such as beef and palm oil, from suppliers in countries with rainforests. Environmentalists claim that these large purchases encourage ranchers to burn down rainforests to create feedlots for beef cattle.

The fast-food industry has also acquired palm oil and coffee from tropical nations in Latin America, Sub-Saharan Africa and Southeast Asia. Environmentalists argue that the demand for these products encourages planters in these areas to level rainforests to create agricultural land for growing coffee and planting palm trees. As rainforests are home to an estimated half of all the earth's species, the destruction of the forests for farming and other uses, such as logging, has eliminated the habitats of many flora and fauna and harmed indigenous peoples who live in the rainforest.

Mike Roselle, one of the founders of the environmental advocacy organization Earth First!, wrote an article on how beef imports from Central America harmed the rainforest. He began speaking at rallies on what he called the 'Hamburger Connection' and its threat to rainforests.[4] While on a speaking tour, he formed a loose coalition of about 30 local environmental groups that were concerned about the rainforest. He identified Burger King as having contracts with a Costa Rican beef supplier. In April 1983 Roselle held a demonstration in front of a Burger King outlet in San Francisco and then launched a national boycott of the company – the world's second-largest hamburger chain. Burger King brushed off the accusations, claiming that only 2 per cent of its beef came from rainforest areas.

Out of these boycotts emerged the Rainforest Action Network (RAN) in 1985. Its goal was to inform the American public about the plight of rainforests and the peoples who lived in them. Burger King remained RAN's primary target and its revenue declined by a reported 12 per cent. Since 1967 Burger King had been owned by the Pillsbury Company, and in 1986 RAN held a major demonstration at a Pillsbury board meeting in Minneapolis. At the time discussions were under way between Pillsbury and the British conglomerate Grand Metropolitan, which was acquiring the American food giant. When the deal went through, in 1987, new management was hired for Burger King and the company cancelled $35 million of contracts from beef producers in Costa Rica, announcing that it had stopped importing rainforest beef. The cancellation caused havoc in Costa Rica, which lost 60 per cent of its beef exports.[5]

Environmental groups went after other hamburger chains, most of which eliminated direct purchases of beef from countries with rainforests, but the loss of rainforests continued. Between 1996 and 2008, more than 15 per cent of the Amazon rainforest in Brazil was cleared for agricultural use – 75 per cent specifically for cattle ranching. By 2008 the Amazon was home to more than 80 million cattle. Fast-food establishments in countries with rainforests continued to purchase beef ranched on their own deforested land. Beef not consumed in Brazil is mainly exported to Europe.

In April 2006 Greenpeace released a report claiming that McDonald's and other companies were destroying rainforests by purchasing chickens fed on soy beans farmed on deforested land in the Amazon rainforest. It was estimated that McDonald's acquired 50 per cent of the poultry served in its European outlets from this source. Activists demonstrated at McDonald's restaurants dressed in chicken suits. McDonald's worked with other companies also named in the report and in July 2006 announced that they were collectively ending the purchase of chicken fed on soy grown in newly deforested areas of the Amazon rainforest. Greenpeace subsequently praised McDonald's for taking this action.[6]

Palm oil is another product that has contributed to the destruction of the rainforest, particularly in Southeast Asia. Less than half of the world's production of palm oil is produced under an environmental policy known as 'No Deforestation, No Peat, and No Exploitation'. RAN has charged fast-food companies with using 'Conflict Palm Oil' in making french fries, and doughnut companies such as Krispy Kreme, Dunkin' Donuts and Tim Hortons use palm oil or palm-oil blends for frying. As a result of consumer pressure brought about by RAN and other environmental groups, Dunkin' Donuts, Krispy Kreme and other companies have agreed to switch to other oils. Other fast-food chains, such as Yum! Brands, Domino's, Wendy's, Carl's Jr. and Dairy Queen, ranked bottom in the Union of Concerned Scientists' palm-oil scorecard in 2015. Yum! Brands subsequently pledged to acquire their palm oil from sources that do not contribute to deforestation by the end of 2017. Their commitment, however, did not apply to their suppliers.[7]

Fast-food chains sell lots of coffee, virtually all of it sourced from tropical countries. Fresh-brewed coffee has always been a key factor in the success of Dunkin' Donuts. In 1999 the chain announced the sale of their 8 billionth cup of coffee since opening in 1950. Starbucks is currently the largest retailer of speciality coffee in the world, with more than 15,000 stores in 55 countries. McDonald's launched the 'McCafé', a coffeehouse-style chain, in 1993. As of 2014 there were about 1,300 McCafés and more are in the planning stage. Their coffee is typically grown on vast plantations in tropical and semi-tropical areas of Africa, Asia and Latin America. The environmental costs of coffee are high, as forests are cleared for its culture, pesticides are used extensively and intensive cultivation has depleted the soil.

In an attempt to stop the destruction of rainforests, organizations have developed voluntary programmes that certify and label commodities, such as palm oil and coffee, as not coming from recently cleared tropical land. The same organizations publicly criticize companies that continue to use products from non-certified suppliers.

Eco-Fast Food?

Fast-food companies have responded to environmental issues by modifying their packaging; redesigning unsightly buildings; changing their suppliers; and making their outlets 'greener'. There has been an upsurge of interest in creating more environmentally friendly fast-food establishments. Chains such as Burgerville in Oregon and Washington use alternative energy sources, serve more local ingredients and offer more vegetarian items. Rather than handing out a toy, Burgerville includes a packet of garden seeds in its kids' meals. Other chains encourage cyclists to use drive-through facilities.

Some fast-food businesses have begun to use renewable energy sources, such as solar power and wind turbines, to help decrease their dependence on the power grid. Research has shown that restaurants could cut 50 per cent of their power needs by using more energy-efficient appliances. Burgerville, for example, employs wind power for its electrical needs. In 2010 Burger King unveiled a new energy-efficient restaurant in Waghäusel, Germany. It uses renewable energy for about one-third of its electricity needs, and has greatly reduced its overall energy use, thereby sub-stantially reducing both energy costs and emissions.

Many fast-food companies have attempted to lower their carbon footprint. McDonald's, for instance, has made strides in key areas, including product offerings and managing its supply chain. Chipotle Mexican Grill, an American chain that also has about 1,000 outlets in the UK, Canada, Germany and France, is recognized as an industry leader when it comes to sustainable practices and sourcing. Sustainability efforts in the fast-food industry range from promoting healthy food choices like salads, carrot sticks and low-fat milk to using green building techniques and sourcing sustainable ingredients and materials.

New eco-fast-food restaurants are popping up around the world. Amanda's Feel Good Fresh Food restaurant in Berkeley, California, was launched in 2006 by Amanda West and survived in this highly competitive field for only a few years. It served naturally raised beef (in smaller-than-standard portion sizes), freshly made sodas sweetened without corn syrup, baked sweet-potato fries and salads. All packaging was biodegradable and could be disposed of in receptacles along with food waste for composting.

Elevation Burgers, launched by Hans Hess in the u.s. in 2005, is a 'fast casual' franchise restaurant chain with about fifteen locations. Its hamburgers are made with 100 per cent organic beef, and it offers a variety of vegetarian options. The outlets make use of sustainable materials such as bamboo and are designed to be as energy efficient as possible. The corporate headquarters are in Arlington, Virginia.

In 2010 Otarian, a small chain launched in London, New York and Australia, served low-carbon-emission vegetarian fare in its fast-casual restaurants. The menu included vege-tarian burgers, wraps and flatbreads, curries, pasta dishes, soups, salads and desserts. Otarian's 'Eco2tarian Labelling' compared the greenhouse-gas emissions of the ingredients in its dishes with similar ones containing meat, fish or egg. The small chain was widely praised for its attempt to make its customers aware of the environmental consequences of the foods they ate, but it fared badly and most outlets closed.

Perhaps the most environmentally conscious fast-food chain is Max, Sweden's first hamburger chain. Founded in 1968, Max pioneered a lower-fat menu, uses locally produced beef and chicken, and was the first restaurant chain to provide carbon labelling for its meals. In 2008 the chain began to label all products with their climate impact, which gives customers the ability to choose food that has a lower impact on the environment. Customers started ordering more non-beef burgers; sales of low-carbon burgers, such as their veggie Greenburgare, jumped by 16 per cent. Max offsets the environmental impact of its operations by planting trees in Africa.[8] The chain now has outlets in Denmark, Norway and the United Arab Emirates.

Fast-food firms have reduced the amount of waste in their corporate operations. For many companies, the goal is to have zero waste going to landfills. To achieve this, they have instituted or intensified composting, recycling and other practices. While these efforts are welcome, they affect only a small fraction of the total waste produced by their outlets and franchises.

Eco-friendly Designs

Fast-food chains have also altered their architectural designs to incorporate the latest environmental technology. The new eco-friendly fast-food restaurants have greatly reduced their energy consumption; some have solar panels integrated into their design. In 2009 Burger King launched an ambitious plan to make over most of its outlets by installing new technology and building materials that would reduce gas consumption by 52 per cent and electricity by 90 per cent.

The u.s. Green Building Council certifies structures that promote 'environmentally responsible, profitable and healthy places to live and work' as part of their Leadership in Energy and Environmental Design (LEED) programme. While many fast-food outlets have made environmental innovations, as of 2013, fewer than twenty fast-food restaurants in America had received LEED certification. Large chains, such as Dunkin' Donuts, Subway, McDonald's, Arby's, Starbucks and Yum! Brands, have one or more buildings with LEED certification.

The McDonald's LEED outlet in Chicago includes a vegetative green roof, a storm-water management system and Energy Star-rated kitchen equipment. It uses an estimated 25 per cent less energy than their other outlets of the same size.

Most fast-food chains require that franchisees change the outlet's design every few years to meet company specifications. Constant rebranding keeps the company's image fresh, telling consumers that there's always something new and innovative on the way. Rather than making only cosmetic changes, McDonald's sought advice on how to make its operation more environmentally friendly. In 1990 the company created an alliance with the Environmental Defense Fund (EDF) that led to the switch from polystyrene to paper products and a programme to encourage recycling. McDonald's claims to have eliminated more than 300 million pounds of packaging, recycled 1 million tons of corrugated boxes and reduced waste by 30 per cent between 1990 and 2010.[9] The collaboration between McDonald's and the EDF has continued, spawning additional programmes and partnerships. For instance, McDonald's requires that its meat and poultry suppliers pass an annual animal welfare audit conducted by the EDF. In collaboration with Conservation International, McDonald's developed a scorecard to measure and reduce the water, energy, air and waste impacts of its bakery, beef, poultry, pork and potato suppliers. In addition the chain has purchased more than $4 billion of recycled materials for its own operations. As a result of these efforts, McDonald's has garnered a good deal of positive press coverage.

Fast-food companies are experimenting with greener packaging. Yum! Brands claims that its fast-food companies, including KFC and Taco Bell, use napkins made from 100 per cent recycled content. Their drink-cup carriers are also manufactured with recycled content. KFC has introduced reusable food containers for side dishes, such as mashed potatoes, green beans and coleslaw. In 2010 Greener Package (GP), an organization devoted to sustainable packaging, gave KFC an award for significantly reducing the environmental footprint of their packaging. The container lids are embossed with the words 'KFC Reusable, Microwave & Top Rack Dishwasher Safe'. The container requires 25 per cent less energy to produce than the previous package, and generates 50 per cent less greenhouse gases, according to GP.[10] KFC proudly announced that it planned to cut total energy consumption by 10 per cent during the period 2005–15.[11] The company has yet to announce whether it has been successful in achieving this projected reduction.

McDonald's UK claims to have greatly improved its carbon efficiency by investing in low-energy hand dryers, LED lights and energy-saving kitchen equipment. For these efforts, the company was awarded the Carbon Trust Standard in 2010. McDonald's UK hamburgers are supplied by Esca Food Solutions, which won the UK Food Manufacturing Excellence Awards for its burgers in 2007. McDonald's UK announced in 2010 that it was launching a three-year study into reducing the carbon emissions caused by the cattle used in its burgers. The study's results have yet to be released.

These steps are welcome, but fast-food chains contribute indirectly to massive environmental degradation through meat, seafood and poultry acquired from suppliers. Most companies depend on animal feedlots and slaughterhouses that produce vast amounts of waste, which greatly contributes to pollution. Fast-food companies do not operate ranches or meatpacking facilities, but many environmentalists believe that fast-food companies should be held responsible for the actions of their suppliers, particularly those who supply meat and poultry.

6
MEAT

In the early 1990s Will Dana, an editor at *Rolling Stone* magazine, came up with a story idea: a look at America through its fast food. Fellow editor Bob Love liked the idea and knew just the person to write it: Eric Schlosser, an investigative journalist who had published a long exposé in the *Atlantic Monthly* on the transformation of California's agriculture. Schlosser signed up, and in 1997 he began his investigation. He spent a year researching the rise and influence of the fast-food industry after the Second World War, its influences on the American agricultural system, and its promotional campaigns targeting children.

Schlosser's three-part series, 'Fast Food Nation', was published in *Rolling Stone* beginning in 1998. His book of the same name based on these articles was released in January 2001. It was a surprise bestseller, with more than 1.6 million copies sold within a few years of its publication.

Schlosser raised many issues related to fast food, but among the more shocking to readers was his description of working conditions in the meatpacking industry. Meat-packers had managed to operate under the radar for decades. Although no major meatpacking plant allowed Schlosser to visit, workers in the industry were willing to talk to him. He was stunned by the conditions they described – the abuse of their fellow workers, the deterioration of safety standards and the cruelty to animals. One result of these practices, reported Schlosser, was that meatpackers 'facilitated the introduction of deadly pathogens, such as *E. coli* 0157:H7, into America's hamburger meat'.[1]

Reviewers and pundits proclaimed *Fast Food Nation* one of the most influential books ever published about the American food system. It has gone through 85 printings and has been published in fifteen languages. The British edition was titled *Fast Food Nation: What the All-American Meal Is Doing to the World* (2001); the German edition was subtitled 'die dunkle Seite von McFood & Co.' ('the dark side of McFood and Co.'). The book inspired a film of the same name, which premiered at the Cannes Film Festival in 2006, and *Food, Inc.*, a documentary released in 2008.

Despite the popularity of his book and films, little has changed. When Schlosser wrote an afterword for the tenth-anniversary publication of *Fast Food Nation*, he despaired, 'I'd love to report that the book is out of date, that the many problems it describes have been solved, and that the Golden Arches are now the symbol of a fallen empire, like the pyramids at Giza. Sadly, that is not the case.'[2]

Background

Adulterated meat has generated attention in Europe and the United States for centuries. The German-born chemist Frederick Accum included a chapter titled the 'Disgusting Practice of Rendering Butcher's Meat, Fish, and Poultry,

Unwholesome' in his *Treatise on Adulterations of Food, and Culinary Poisons.* Accum's book generated excitement throughout Europe and America. Vegetarians jumped on the anti-meat campaign and regularly reported on adulterated and poisonous beef, pork and poultry products and the negative consequences of eating meat. It wasn't until 1875 that the British Parliament passed the Sale of Foods and Drugs Act, which made the adulteration of food and the sale of unwholesome meat illegal. In the u.s. similar bills were introduced into Congress, but none passed.

Meat had held a central place in the American diet since colonial times. By 1900 a survey estimated that Americans consumed, on average, 136 pounds (61.7 kg) of meat annually. Virtually every American ate meat. When Upton Sinclair published *The Jungle* (1906), an exposé of the American meatpacking industry, it caused a public uproar against the meat industry, which ensured the passage of the Pure Food and Drug Act and the Meat Inspection Act by u.s. Congress. The Pure Food and Drug Act created what would become the Food and Drug Administration (FDA), which has been charged with ensuring the safety of the nation's food supply – except for meat, poultry and eggs. The Meat Inspection Act empowered federal inspectors in the u.s. Department of Agriculture to examine animals before and after slaughter, to be present when diseased animals were destroyed, and to inspect processed products for dangerous chemicals, preservatives or dyes. No meat that had not been inspected could be shipped across state lines. Rules, regulations and inspection programmes were established to ensure compli-ance. Over the following decades, the meatpacking industry gradually improved owing to governmental regulations and inspections. Workers' pay increased; by the 1960s meatpackers were among the highest-paid industrial workers in the United States. Their workers were represented by unions and employee turnover was low.

Beginning in the 1960s, the American meat and poultry industries bore the brunt of the fast-food revolution, which was directly linked to an enormous increase in meat production. Large chains pressurized meatpackers for cheap, uniform products that tasted the same regardless of where they had been produced. In 1982 the American meatpacking industry was deregulated. The unions that represented workers at packing plants were decimated, and strikebreakers were brought in by plant owners to operate slaughterhouses and processing facilities. Wages dropped by 30 per cent and working conditions deteriorated. This was a major victory for the plant owners, who enjoyed lower labour costs, higher production rates and greater profits. Once the unions were out of the picture, immigrant workers, many of whom are undocumented, made fewer complaints to regulatory authorities. The result was that the meatpacking industry now provides the lowest-paid and most demanding, hazardous and exhausting jobs in America.[3] According to the Bureau of Labor Statistics, more than one in four workers in meatpacking plants have suffered a job-related injury or illness.

The meat industry has continually lobbied against regulations for food safety. The Occupational Safety and Health Administration can levy fines on non-compliant meatpackers, but the maximum fine for a human death is only $70,000

– hardly a burden for a meatpacker making millions of dollars a year. The meatpacking industry has also supported so-called 'veggie libel laws', which forbid the defamation of agricultural products and place the burden of proof on the party being sued. When Oprah Winfrey, a talk-show host, badmouthed beef on her hugely popular television show in 1996, she was sued by cattle ranchers in a Texas court. Although Winfrey won the case, the meatpacking industry had proved that it could threaten critics – even popular television stars – with expensive lawsuits.

Animal Feeding Operations

During the Second World War an agricultural labour shortage hit the u.s. just when farms needed to step up production. More food was required for the 11.5 million u.s. military personnel and to help feed America's allies in Europe and Asia. To ramp up production, farmers began confining cattle, pigs and poultry to large buildings or outdoor pens for most of their lives, and feeding them a scientifically formulated diet. The animals could be fed more easily and quickly, and their manure more efficiently collected for conversion into fertilizer. Confining animals also reduced losses to predators and illness. Raising livestock in confined areas made sense even after the war: by 1960, 26.7 per cent of cattle in Kansas were raised on large feedlots; by 1975, 87.6 per cent of cattle were housed on feedlots for part of their lives.

Fast-food chains typically acquire their meat indirectly from industrial feedlots called animal feeding operations (AFOs). Large cattle concentrated animal feeding operations

(CAFOS) can feed as many as 100,000 animals at one time. Feedlots are factory-like buildings or open-air pens where food animals are kept. Meat animals are typically raised from birth on farms and then shipped to feedlots or other facilities that ready cattle, pigs and chickens for market. Cattle usually have their horns cut off or chemically reduced in size to prevent the animals from goring one another in the small, confined space. In the feedlots the animals are fed a special diet to fatten them before they are shipped to slaughter.

Broiler chickens are raised in hatcheries, farms and AFOS; they are sent to be slaughtered five to nine weeks later, when they reach market weight. Broilers are usually housed in factory-like buildings of about 20,000 square ft (1,858 square m; 40 ft wide and 500 ft long, or 12.2 × 152.4 m). Large operations can process 600,000 broilers per year. Because birds in confined areas tend to peck each other to death, their beaks are partially seared off. Antibiotics (or antimicrobial medicines) are administered to prevent disease and increase growth. The introduction of antibiotics also had an impact on laying hens. As a result of such changes, egg production soared; some hens began to lay as many as 300 eggs per year. The size of henhouses sometimes increased to 100,000 layers, and profits soared.

During the 1950s pig farmers moved their swine off pastures and into buildings, where the temperature, lighting and feed could be closely controlled, thus creating the ideal environment for fattening the animals to their maximum weight in the shortest time. Pigs raised in feeding operations progress through three main stages: sows are naturally or artificially inseminated; the piglets are weaned at two to three weeks and then fed for six weeks before being shipped to another operation, where they are fed a high-calorie diet until they reach market weight. The pigs are then sent to slaughterhouses.

Although animal feeding operations are usually family-owned and operated, they rely more and more on hired labour. The farms operate on efficiencies of scale; as a result, American meat production has shifted to larger operations. The increasing volume of animals caused large meat processors to grow even bigger; small ones closed as their distribution channels dried up. These operations are closely connected with large food processors, which have become highly concentrated as well. In 2005, for instance, four multinational meatpackers – Tyson Foods, Cargill, Brazil-based JBS and National Beef – controlled about 80 per cent of all beef cattle slaughtered in the U.S. The same companies, plus the Chinese-owned Smithfield Foods, control 60 per cent of America's pork. The broiler chicken industry is controlled by four companies, Tyson Foods being the largest.[4]

The manure generated by animal feeding operations is considerable and requires proper disposal. Typically, untreated pig and cattle waste is stored in above-ground, open-air earthen pits or ponds called lagoons. Poultry producers typically use dry-waste systems, where the manure is scraped out of buildings or collected on conveyor belts and then moved to storage sites. When the waste decomposes, it is sprayed or spread on farmland to enrich the soil with nutrients such as nitrogen. But improperly managed wastewater from animal feeding operations has generated significant environmental concerns, including nutrient over-enrichment of surface water and groundwater, contamination of drinking water, fish kills and production of methane and other greenhouse gases.

Proponents of animal feeding operations argue that these operations are efficient and safe. Confined livestock is supervised more closely than free-range animals, and diseases can be treated more quickly should they develop. Because animals are given antibiotics and their diet is carefully managed, they gain more weight than free-range animals. Proponents claim that the greater efficiencies of animal feeding operations – which produce more meat and eggs than traditional methods – mean that fewer farm animals are being raised, which has a positive overall effect on the environment. Another argument in their favour is that they have led to lower retail prices for meat and eggs. They also use much less farmland than do traditional livestock operations, and they employ less labour. They have thus freed land and labour for other uses.

Environmental concerns over animal feeding operations have emerged since the 1970s. In general meat production has a much greater impact on the environment than cultivating crops: livestock require more land, feed and energy to raise and transport. Intensive animal farming also requires a tremendous amount of water, and this can lead to water depletion in areas where it is naturally scarce, or in periods of drought. Decreasing consumption of meat, opponents claim, could thus improve the environment. In particular animal feeding operations produce large amounts of animal waste, which is stored in lagoons, some the length of multiple football fields. Unlike human waste, which is treated with chemical and filtration systems before being released into the environment, animal waste is not treated. Typically it decomposes in lagoons before being sprayed on fields as fertilizer.

Lagoons have broken, failed and overflowed, especially during rainstorms. Virtually every state with animal feeding operations has suffered from multiple releases of untreated waste. There have been massive spills with lethal results. In the summer of 1995 heavy rains caused several lagoons to burst in North Carolina. A dyke surrounding an 8-acre pig-waste lagoon at Oceanview Farms in Onslow County burst, spilling an estimated 25 million gallons of liquid pig faeces and urine into neighbouring crop land and two tributaries of the New River. As a result, an estimated 10 million fish died and 364,000 acres of coastal wetlands were closed to shellfish harvesting for several months. Four years later, when Hurricane Floyd hit North Carolina, almost 50 lagoons burst and their waste was released. In 2011 a pig farm near Buckley, Illinois, spilled 200,000 gallons of untreated animal waste into Spring Creek, killing more than 100,000 fish.

Animal waste contains potentially harmful substances: nitrates, heavy metals and micro-pollutants. Traces of steroid hormones, acaricides (which target ticks and mites) and insecticides are released into the environment by animal feeding operations and treated animals in general, and traces have been found in groundwater. Little is known of the processes that govern their transport in soil or how they eventually reach groundwater. As they are widely used in animal husbandry, they have significant impacts on soil.[5] They have been found in low concentrations in the environment, but their presence is persistent and ubiquitous, and this concerns many scientists.

Environmentalists have also targeted animal feeding operations because of the real and potential damage caused by high concentrations of manure-based nutrients, which may result in a loss of groundwater for commercial or recreational use. As the cost of transporting liquid waste is high, it tends to be sprayed on nearby crop land, which can absorb only so much moisture. Excessive waste applications create runoff that ends up in groundwater, streams, rivers and lakes. Nutrients in animal waste contribute to algal blooms; these uncontrolled proliferations of algae deplete the oxygen in the water, resulting in 'dead zones' in lakes and oceans where fish and shellfish cannot survive.

There is also an environmental concern with air pollution: environmentalists claim that large animal feeding operations are the largest single cause of ammonia and other emissions, such as methane, carbon dioxide, hydrogen sulphide and nitrous oxide, variously associated with global warming, ozone depletion and acid deposition. More than 160 gases are known to be emitted from the waste. Ammonia, a toxic, colourless gas with a pungent odour, has been known to travel more than 300 miles (480 km) through the air before being dumped back on to the ground or into the water, where it also contributes to algal blooms. Airborne particulate matter found near animal feeding operations can carry disease-causing bacteria, fungus or other pathogens. Several studies of workers and people who live near AFOs report health problems, including eye irritation, sore throats, coughs, nausea, shortness of breath, fluid in the lungs, headaches, diarrhoea, dizziness, depression, loss of appetite, poor memory and fatigue.

Proponents argue that, when properly located, managed and monitored, animal feeding operations have created production efficiencies in raising animals. They have given farmers the ability to manage animal husbandry much more effectively. These operations provide a reliable, reasonably priced supply of meat, milk and eggs. Advocates also maintain that the economics and concentration of animal feeding operations result in less environmental impact 'per animal' delivered to market. While conceding that environmental concerns have substance, supporters of animal feeding operations see these issues as greatly exaggerated, and stress that improvements are underway. For instance, new systems have been developed for the improved handling of animal waste. The waste can be used to produce methane, which can then be used to fuel machinery.

Thanks in part to fast food, meat consumption is increasing in many countries, particularly in developing countries such as China and Brazil. Factory farming is accelerating as a means of animal production to keep up with increased demand. In 2006 these systems generated 74 per cent of the world's poultry products, 50 per cent of all pork, 43 per cent of beef and 68 per cent of eggs.[6] McDonald's is the largest purchaser of beef in America, and is second only to KFC in its purchase of chickens. As meat consumption is increasing in many parts of the world, observers are concerned about the potential environmental effects.

Antibiotics

Another major shift in animal husbandry occurred with the discovery of antibiotics (or antimicrobial medicines) in the 1930s. Antibiotics, such as tetracycline, penicillin and erythromycin, kill or retard the growth of bacteria. They have been tremendously effective in treating and preventing diseases in humans and animals and are generally considered safe.

The use of antibiotics in farm animals commenced in the 1940s when producers started vaccinating their herds and flocks and testing them regularly for pathogens, hoping to forestall the spread of illness among farm animals. In 1950 scientists at American Cyanamid's Lederle laboratory found that antibiotics could be added to feed – not just administered when disease was already present. Antibiotic-laced chicken and pig feed were quickly adopted.[7] This method was less successful with cattle, as bovines have multiple stomachs that process feed differently, but other means of administering the drugs to cattle were soon developed.

For reasons that are not fully understood, antibiotics in feed accelerate weight gain in animals (about 70 per cent of the total antibiotics now used in America are given to chickens, pigs and cattle in the absence of disease). So the treated animals not only fought off diseases but grew faster, gaining 3 per cent more weight before slaughter – increasing profits for owners. The use of antibiotics increased herd and flock sizes, and per-unit production costs declined. In 1951 the Food and Drug Administration approved the routine addition of penicillin and tetracycline to chicken feed as growth promoters.

Also added to animal feed were vitamins and mineral additives, such as copper, zinc and even arsenic, because of their antimicrobial and growth-stimulating effects. With production costs dropping, many predicted that pork, chicken and beef prices would fall to new lows – a prediction that soon came true.

By the 1990s virtually all commercially raised livestock raised in the United States (except those certified as organic) were routinely administered antibiotics. Concern with these drugs in animal feed first emerged during the 1960s. Scientists found that bacteria that were repeatedly exposed to antibiotics developed resistance, becoming immune to the drugs designed to kill them. As the antibiotics were similar to those used in people, it was feared that using the drugs in animal feed could render existing antibiotics useless when needed to fight infection in humans. These concerns motivated some Americans to lobby for a ban on antibiotic use on farms, arguing that giving animals 'subtherapeutic' doses of antibiotics fosters bacterial resistance in meat-eating humans. Antibiotics are still commonly used in the United States, where about 16 million pounds (72.6 million kg) of antibiotics are administered annually to farm animals – about 30 times more than to humans.[8]

According to the Humane Society of the United States, 'Indiscriminate use of antibiotics may lead to the evolution of resistance by selecting directly for drug-resistant pathogens as well as for mobile genetic elements carrying resistance determinants to both human and nonhuman animal pathogens.' The Centers for Disease Control concluded that the reason for an increase in antibiotic resistance in foodborne diseases in the u.s. 'is because of antibiotic use on the farm'.[9]

Another concern within the medical and scientific communities is that continued routine use of antibiotics in animal feed will create a 'superbug' that is resistant to all known antibiotics, and that it will wreak devastation on people, animals and other life forms. Many organizations, including the American Medical Association and the American Public Health Association, have endorsed efforts to phase out the use of antibiotics as animal feed additives.

Some fast-food companies have also opposed the use of antibiotics by their meat suppliers. Chipotle's beef, poultry and pork comes from suppliers that do not use antibiotics or hormones. Pret A Manger, a British-based fast-casual restaurant chain, has proclaimed that they only use antibiotic-free, preservative-free and hormone-free ingredients. Wendy's has sourced its meat from companies that do not use human antibiotics solely for the purpose of growth promotion in animals. In 2004 Panera Bread, a fast-casual restaurant chain in Canada and the United States, made the decision to serve no chicken, turkey or pork treated with antibiotics. Ten years later, Chick-fil-A, an American chain specializing in chicken sandwiches, announced that they are phasing out purchasing chickens raised with antibiotics. Tyson Foods and Perdue Farms, multinationals that supply much of the chicken to American fast-food chains, sell lines of chicken products from birds that have never been given antibiotics. In 2015 Tyson reported that they have reduced the use of human antibiotics used to treat their chickens by more than 84 per cent since 2011, and Perdue reported that 95 per cent of their chickens were raised without any human antibiotics.

McDonald's announced that they will phase out buying chicken raised with non-therapeutic, medically important antibiotics in their 14,000 u.s. locations by 2017. Their pledge does not include antibiotics given to treat diseases that arise from overcrowded and unsanitary farming conditions. Critics were quick to point out that McDonald's made a similar pledge in 2003: 'McDonald's prohibits the use of antibiotics belonging to classes of compounds approved for use in human medicine when used solely for growth promotion purposes. Growth promotion is defined as the use of antibiotics for any purpose other than disease treatment, control or prevention.' That 2003 pledge, claimed critics, was unfulfilled.[10] The 2015 pledge covers only chicken, not beef or pork, but the move by McDonald's is expected to influence the poultry industry and perhaps eventually the production of other meat.

The European Union banned the use of antibiotics as growth promoters in food animals in 2006, but individual nations have applied the ban selectively. Fast-food chains operating in the European Union have announced that their meat products are from animals raised without antibiotics. McDonald's uk reports that its hamburgers are 100 per cent beef and that they contain no preservatives or added flavours. McDonald's uk's burgers are acquired from Esca Food Solutions, which works closely with 16,000 independent farmers in the uk and Ireland to maintain high standards. (McDonald's also notes that the fish used in Filet-O-Fish and Fish Finger meals are from sustainable fisheries certified by the Marine Stewardship Council.[11])

Animal Welfare and Vegetarian Matters

Animal welfare came to the cultural forefront in the 1970s, when many new organizations focusing on specific aspects of animal welfare, animal rights, vegetarianism and veganism emerged. These diverse groups campaigned against the production and use of animals for fur, and against trapping, hunting, whaling, the killing of dolphins in the fishing industry and the display of animals in zoos and aquariums. Many animal-rights organizations see much to oppose in the fast-food industry, particularly in the meatpacking industry that supports it.

People for the Ethical Treatment of Animals (PETA) claims to be the largest animal rights organization in the world, with more than 3 million members and supporters. It was founded in 1980 by Ingrid Newkirk with the mission of relieving the suffering of animals 'through public education, cruelty investigations, research, animal rescue, legislation, special events, celebrity involvement, and protest campaigns'. PETA maintains that it is inhumane to confine animals in tightly packed pens or cages. It has repeatedly filmed the inhumane treatment of animals in feeding operations and slaughterhouses to publicize these concerns. Other animal-rights organizations have also taken footage of these operations. In response agriculture organizations in the U.S. have supported 'ag-gag' laws making it illegal to film agricultural operations, such as animal feeding operations and slaughterhouses, without permission. As of 2014 two states (Utah and Iowa) have passed ag-gag laws; both have been challenged in court.

PETA targeted McDonald's in 2000 in a 'McCruelty' campaign aimed at changing the way the corporation's suppliers handled chickens. McDonald's was targeted because it is the second largest buyer of chicken in the world, after KFC. PETA members engaged in more than 400 demonstrations against the company, and after two years McDonald's agreed 'to make basic welfare improvements for farmed animals', according to PETA.[12] McDonald's also made a policy decision to purchase eggs only from poultry producers who adopted more humane production practices. McDonald's also introduced vegetarian options after PETA turned the spotlight on them.

PETA released a video in 2004 taken at a slaughterhouse in Moorfield, West Virginia, owned by Pilgrim's Pride, a KFC supplier. The video revealed workers cruelly abusing and killing chickens by throwing them against the walls or kicking them to death, for instance, simply out of boredom with their gruelling work.[13] The renowned veterinary scientist and animal behaviourist Dr Temple Grandin proclaimed the actions shown on the tape 'absolutely atrocious'. Pilgrim's Pride fired several employees and began a workforce training programme aimed at preventing animal cruelty in the future.

PETA Asia Pacific complained about the treatment of chickens in KFC Korea's suppliers in 2005. The *Seoul Times* reported that PETA's exposé 'revealed that workers were stomping on live birds, tearing their heads off, spitting tobacco in their eyes, and spray-painting their faces'. KFC Korea ignored recommendations for animal welfare improvements by its own Animal Welfare Advisory Council, resulting in the resignation of several members.[14]

PETA once again took on McDonald's, claiming that the outdated slaughter methods used by the company's chicken suppliers resulted in needless suffering. PETA stated that 'McDonald's has the responsibility – and the ability – to reduce abuse by demanding that its U.S. and Canadian suppliers use a less cruel slaughter method.' In one demonstration in Chicago, the comedian and animal-rights activist Andy Dick dressed up as Ronald McDonald and wielded a prop cleaver to 'scare' McDonald's management into changing company policy. Afterwards Dick said, 'if kids knew how chickens were mutilated for McNuggets, they'd burst into tears every time Ronald McDonald showed his face – and that may well happen when they see what this clown has to say about it.'[15]

The Physicians Committee for Responsible Medicine released a 30-second anti-McDonald's commercial depicting a corpse lying in a morgue, a partially eaten hamburger still in his lifeless hand. A McDonald's golden arch logo appears on the corpse's feet along with the words, 'I was lovin' it.' The voice-over says, 'High cholesterol, high blood pressure, heart attacks. Tonight, make it vegetarian.'[16] Few television stations aired the commercial, but the advertisement received extensive visibility on television news programmes, in newspapers and online. By 2015, 1.7 million viewers had watched it on YouTube. McDonald's, the National Restaurant Association and others condemned the advertisement, calling it 'irresponsible'.

On the subject of irresponsibility, Google's new YouTube Kids app features extensive fast-food advertising. McDonald's has its own 'branded channel', where it advertises extensively.

One promotion dubbed 'The Unapologetic Big Mac' warns: 'All vegetarians, foodies and gastronauts, kindly avert your eyes.' The camera then turns to a Big Mac and the narrator announces, 'You can't get juiciness like this from soy or quinoa.' It focuses on the lettuce and announces, 'Nor will this ever be kale.' The company also paid for large billboards directing readers to 'Go Beefetarian' and buy the company's triple cheeseburger.[17] The sign didn't report that their triple cheeseburger had 510 calories, 27 grams of fat and 1150 mg of sodium.[18]

A coalition of U.S. organizations – the Center for Digital Democracy, Campaign for a Commercial-free Childhood, the American Academy of Child and Adolescent Psychiatry, the Center for Science in the Public Interest, Children Now, the Consumer Federation of America, Consumer Watchdog, Corporate Accountability International and Public Citizen – have filed a complaint with the Federal Trade Commission (FTC) claiming that these advertisements were excessive and deceptive, violating the FTC's restrictions against marketing junk food to children.[19]

Beef Flavouring

Many animal rights advocates are vegetarians or vegans. Vegetarians, who eat no meat, poultry or seafood, and vegans, who do not eat animals or animal products, such as milk, eggs and cheese, have been among the most ardent opponents of fast-food culture. Vegetarians of all stripes have campaigned against intensive animal feeding operations, slaughterhouse and meatpacking procedures and fast-food chains.

In 1990, in response to criticism of the cholesterol content of their fries, McDonald's announced with considerable fanfare that the chain would discontinue the use of beef fat for cooking fries and switch to vegetable oil (with 'added natural flavorings'). In 2001 vegetarians initiated a class-action suit against McDonald's, claiming that the company had concealed its continued use of an animal product in the frying oil. Similar suits were filed in four other states. When the news of the American lawsuit reached India, there was outrage among vegetarians. A Hindu fundamentalist group ransacked a McDonald's in a Bombay suburb, and another group of demonstrators surrounded one of the chain's locations and smeared cow dung on a statue of Ronald McDonald. The company denied that anything other than 100 per cent vegetable oil was used to cook fries in its outlets in India.

McDonald's management admitted that 'minuscule' amounts of beef flavouring had been added to the oil. In the settlement McDonald's agreed to donate $10 million to vegetarian, Hindu and other groups, such as Muslims who eat meat only in accordance with halal procedures. Funds approved by the court were distributed to twelve organizations, including two Muslim groups that were not vegetarian. Two other groups that received funds were the Department of Nutrition at Tufts University, which critics claimed was opposed to vegetarianism, and the Nutrition Department at the University of North Carolina, chaired by Dr Steven Zeisel, 'a notorious animal experimenter', claimed a vegetarian.[20]

McDonald's also published an apology online, stating that 'We regret that we did not provide these customers with complete information, and we sincerely apologize for any hardship that these miscommunications have caused.' McDonald's also made it clear, however, that they had never stated that their french fries were a vegetarian food.[21]

Pink Slime, Horsemeat, Stinky Beef and Seasoned Beef

When meatpackers process animal carcasses, they strive to get every bit of usable tissue off the skeleton. The traditional equipment for scraping meat from bones sometimes removed small fragments of bone as well, and occasionally pieces of the animals' spinal columns. The latter became a major problem with the emergence of mad cow disease – bovine spongiform encephalopathy (BSE), a degenerative brain disease seen in cattle, and its human counterpart, variant Creutzfeldt–Jakob disease (vCJD). BSE, first discovered in the UK in 1986, devastated the English cattle industry and killed 176 people in Britain. It is thought that people developed vCJD after consuming undercooked meat contaminated with BSE, and that the most likely vector was 'mechanically recovered meat', especially brain, spinal cord and other organ tissue.

In 2001 Eldon N. Roth, an inventor and founder of Beef Products (today IBP) in South Dakota, discovered a new way to remove edible pieces of meat, fat and gristle from bones by using a centrifuge. These trimmings were then liquefied and used for making canned pet food. Roth thought that this substance could also be added to ground beef for hamburgers. To be on the safe side, Roth injected the scraps with ammonium hydroxide (NH_4OH), which killed potential pathogens, such as *Salmonella* and *E. Coli*.

Ammonium hydroxide was (and is) approved for use in food by the U.S. Federal Safety and Inspection Service.

Roth called his new product 'lean, finely textured beef' (LFTB). It was approved for human consumption by the U.S. Department of Agriculture (USDA), and in 2001 Beef Products began to sell ground beef with LFTB. The combination had several obvious advantages: it was cheaper and leaner than normal hamburger, and it tasted the same. What's more, it could be labelled 'all beef' because, technically, it was. LFTB quickly became an important ingredient in ground beef sold in American supermarkets and fast-food chains, and it was distributed to schools through the federal National School Lunch Program. By 2009 about 70 per cent of ground beef sold in America contained LFTB.

When Michael Moss, a *New York Times* reporter, was researching an article on food safety, he filed a freedom of information request with the USDA regarding the safety of American beef. Among the many documents he received was a copy of an email from Gerald Zirnstein, a microbiologist working for the USDA. Zirnstein had been tasked with examining the make-up of ground beef to determine whether it met federal regulations. In some ground beef that he tested, he found LFTB. In 2002 he wrote an email stating that he did not consider LFTB to be ground beef, and that he saw allowing its inclusion in 'ground beef to be a form of fraudulent labeling'. Zirnstein referred to LFTB as 'pink slime'.

Moss's article on food safety was published in December 2009, and included a quotation from Zirnstein's email mentioning pink slime. Nothing dangerous had been uncovered about LFTB in the eight years that it had been used, and Moss's article generated little interest. This changed with the British chef Jamie Oliver's television show *Food Revolution*, which aired on 11 April 2011 in the U.S. Oliver revealed the facts about pink slime, calling it 'shit' (the word was bleeped out) and claiming that it was not fit for human consumption. The term 'pink slime' went viral on the Internet. Newspapers and television programmes picked up the story, and a chorus of objections were heard around the country. Facing potential public relations disasters, fast-food chains, including McDonald's, Taco Bell and Burger King, quietly suspended their use of LFTB in January 2012. Others followed. Wendy's proudly announced that they had never used hamburger meat containing pink slime. Despite the uproar, fast-food sales did not suffer.

The pink slime brouhaha was just one of many meat-related controversies that have haunted the fast-food industry. The public reaction was based on a deep concern about the safety of meat in the modern industrial food system in general and the fast-food industry in particular, and consumers have good reason to be worried.

Another beef scandal was the one involving Taco Bell and its seasoned beef. In 2011 an Alabama law firm, Beasley, Allen, Crow, Methvin, Portis & Miles, filed a class-action lawsuit against Taco Bell chain for false advertising. What Taco Bell called seasoned beef was actually just 36 per cent meat, according to the law firm's analysis. The rest consisted of extenders, binders and preservatives, including wheat, oats, water, modified corn starch, sodium phosphate, soy lecithin, autolysed yeast extract, maltodrextrin, soy bean oil, flavourings and other ingredients. If this were the case, they argued, it would violate U.S. Department of Agriculture guidelines that require 'beef' products to be at least 70 per cent beef. Taco Bell denied that their advertising was misleading, and claimed that their seasoned beef was 88 per cent beef, with the addition of a 'secret formula' consisting of water, sugar and spices. Taco Bell carried out a major campaign on Facebook offering a free 'crunchy seasoned beef taco' to users. It became the largest promotion involving complimentary tacos in fast-food history.[22] Taco Bell also threatened to counter-sue the law firm and its client. The firm dropped its lawsuit, claiming that Taco Bell had made 'changes in marketing and product disclosure'.[23]

Yet another crisis overtook KFC China and other fast-food chains in China. On 23 November 2012 the State Television station in Shanghai reported that two of KFC's poultry suppliers had used excessive antiviral drugs and hormones to make their animals grow faster. KFC sales in China plunged 37 per cent in a month. It was later revealed that KFC had been testing its poultry supply since 2010 and knew that it contained high levels of drugs, but used the chicken anyway and did not inform the authorities. The company reassured the public that it had expanded its testing programme, and cut 1,000 small chicken farms from its supply network, shifting to major companies, such as the Shanghai Husi Food Corporation, a subsidiary of OSI Group of Aurora, Illinois.

KFC China sales had just started to recover when Dragon TV in Shanghai broke the news, on 21 July 2014, that Husi had sold beef, pork and chicken with expired safety dating to KFC, McDonald's, Pizza Hut and Dicos, a fast-food chain specializing in chicken that is owned by Taiwan's Ting Hsin International Group. A television clip showed workers in Shanghai Husi's plant picking up meat scraps from the factory floor with their bare hands, and reported that employees had mixed 'stinky beef' past its expiration date with fresh meat. Reports later surfaced that Burger King, Papa John's Pizza, Subway and Starbucks locations in Shanghai had also received products from Husi, as had McDonald's outlets in Tokyo and Hong Kong. The fast-food chains immediately withdrew all products received from Husi, and apologized to the public for the scandal.

Simultaneous with the stinky beef scandal in China was the horsemeat scandal in Europe. Although most of the horsemeat was sold in supermarkets, some was found in products made by companies that supplied beef to Taco Bell and Burger King in the UK and Ireland. In January 2013 horse DNA was found in beefburger patties sold in groceries. In some cases the horsemeat was almost 30 per cent of the entire burger. Some horsemeat originated at a Romanian-based slaughterhouse, and it was widely used throughout England and Ireland. Burger King UK admitted that traces of horsemeat had been found at one of its Irish suppliers. It then changed suppliers. Other fast-food chains were required to deny that their burgers contained horsemeat.

An independent investigation in 2008 of the content of the hamburgers sold in eight fast-food chains found that the actual meat content (defined as skeletal muscle) ranged from 2.1 per cent to 14.8 per cent. In addition to skeletal muscle, the study found connective tissue, blood vessels, peripheral nerve adipose tissue, plant material, cartilage, bone and

Sarcocystis parasites. Their conclusion was that 'Fast food hamburgers are comprised of little meat (median, 12.1%). Approximately half of their weight is made up of water.'[24]

Forbidden Fast Foods

Many religions have dietary codes, with forbidden foods, fast days, holiday specialities and dining customs. When people who follow religious laws encounter fast-food chains, conflict sometimes results. The Jewish dietary laws, known as *kashruth*, were outlined in the Old Testament books of Leviticus and Deuteronomy and have been amplified by centuries of scholarly interpretation. The laws fall into three basic categories: prohibition of the consumption of blood, of certain categories of animals (such as swine or shellfish), and of combining milk and meat products. Animal slaughter must be carried out under very stringent conditions, and the handling, processing and packaging of all food must take place under rabbinic supervision. The Union of Orthodox Jewish Congregations is the best-known certifier of kosher foods in the United States. Foods certified by this group are identified with a symbol consisting of a letter U inside a letter O.

In Israel most fast-food chains, such as Burger King, KFC, McDonald's and Sbarro, have kosher restaurants. In the U.S. chains have kosher-certified outlets. Many Baskin-Robbins outlets are kosher, but a few flavours served at kosher outlets are not, and each store has a sign indicating which are kosher. Dunkin' Donuts, Krispy Kreme, Nathan's and Subway have kosher outlets. Most are located in areas with large Jewish populations, such as New York City.

The laws of Islam, called *sharia*, are set down in the Qur'an and other holy works. The dietary laws identify foods that may be eaten – called *halal*, or permissible – and those that may not, which are classified as *haram*, or forbidden. The manner in which animals are to be slaughtered for consumption is also delineated.

In the U.S. KFC has served halal chicken in some locations for years; many halal outlets are in urban areas with large populations of Muslims.[25] Other fast-food chains, such as Subway, that operate in the Muslim world are certified as halal. Halal meat served in fast-food establishments has become an issue in several European countries. In France the hamburger chain Quick has opened franchises that serve halal foods in order to attract customers from the country's 6 million Muslims. Non-Muslim mayors and political leaders from left to right on the political spectrum vigorously objected to the outlets that did not sell non-halal options.[26]

In the UK halal food is sold in many Subway outlets. In 2010 McDonald's UK admitted that some of its 1,200 British outlets had sold some chicken that had undergone halal procedures. It upgraded its practices to prevent this from happening. Christian groups complained that menu items with halal foods were not identified as such, and they requested that companies clearly label halal foods giving customers the option to choose what they preferred.[27]

Beginning in 2000, McDonald's outlets in areas with high concentrations of Muslims in the U.S., such as Dearborn, Michigan, sold clearly identified Halal Chicken McNuggets and Halal McChicken sandwiches, but discontinued them in 2013 due to lawsuits by Muslims who claimed that McDonald's was selling non-halal food labelled as 'halal'.[28]

Vegetarians, World Hunger and Fast Food

Along with animal rights and dietary laws, another objection to meat consumption at fast-food chains is world hunger. In her book *Diet for a Small Planet* (1971), Frances Moore Lappé argued that feeding vegetable protein to animals rather than directly to people was a waste of scarce resources at a time when many around the world were starving or suffering from serious nutritional deficiencies. Since large-scale intensive livestock operations are constantly producing more meat and dairy products, world hunger activists have bemoaned the fact that countless acres of crop land are used to grow food to feed animals rather than people. An estimated 90 per cent of the world's soybeans and 33 per cent of its grain are consumed as animal feed. If people in high-income nations stopped eating meat, claim many advocates, the rest of the world could be better nourished, and crop land could be preserved, thus improving the environment.

Yum! Brands, the owner of Taco Bell, KFC and Pizza Hut, has raised money to fight world hunger. In 2007 it launched the World Hunger Relief programme to support the efforts of the United Nations World Food Programme (WFP) and other hunger relief agencies. In 2009 KFC teamed up with WFP to raise money for food assistance programmes in Somalia, India, Rwanda, Colombia and Ethiopia. As of 2015 WFP has generated an estimated $600 million in cash and food to alleviate hunger, making it the world's largest private-sector hunger-relief effort.

Despite such meritorious efforts, an estimated 805 million go hungry around the world today, according to the United Nations. This number will likely increase during the following decades as climate change disrupts the world's agricultural patterns, fresh water supplies decline, and the world's population increases from 7 billion to 9.6 billion by 2050. The vast increase in meat production during the past several decades has been directly linked to the rise of the fast-food industry. Due in part to the projected global expansion of the fast-food industry, world meat production is expected to rise from 275 million tons to 475 million tons by 2050.[29] Where the additional farmland will come from to grow crops to feed so many additional animals is unknown. Hunger activists, vegetarians, vegans, animal rights proponents and many environmentalists argue that it's time to stop eating fast foods containing beef, pork, chicken and farmed fish, and begin working on meatless alternatives.

Criticism and Corporate Responses

Unlike animal feeding operations and meat-processing facilities, fast-food chains sell their products directly to the public. Public disclosures about animal welfare, ecological problems, health issues and working conditions in multinational supply chains can damage a company's public image and hurt its bottom line.

Chains have frequently responded defensively to criticism of their suppliers. When Eric Schlosser published *Chew on*

This: Everything You Don't Want to Know about Fast Food (2006), his book for teenagers, and the movie *Fast Food Nation* (2006) was released, large food corporations and their trade groups, such as the National Council of Chain Restaurants, launched a coalition called 'Best Food Nation' intended to counter 'critics of our food system' who promoted agendas 'using information that is inaccurate, misleading and incomplete'. After sending out press releases and publishing a few online articles praising the food industry and demonizing Schlosser, the 'Best Food Nation' coalition quietly disappeared. McDonald's and other companies partly funded a website called TCS Daily, which published an article attacking Schlosser; two days later the article was removed. All these efforts accomplished was to give *Chew on This* and *Fast Food Nation* more visibility.

Fast-food chains have learned to respond more positively. McDonald's has regularly launched media blitzes promoting new, healthy menu offerings and spotlighting workers who have moved up the corporate ladder at the company. Chains have responded to pressure from animal-rights advocates by requiring that meat processors handle and slaughter animals more humanely. After PETA and other animal-rights groups staged protests at McDonald's, the company hired Dr Temple Grandin, a professor of animal science at Colorado State University and one of the nation's foremost experts on animal welfare, to create new procedures for the slaughterhouses that provide the chain's meat. McDonald's threatened to stop buying meat from suppliers that mistreated animals, and auditors were hired to guarantee compliance. They make unannounced visits to slaughterhouses to make sure that animals are properly handled and stunned before being killed. The system that Grandin devised was supported by the meatpacking industry, and other fast-food chains, such as Burger King and Wendy's, required their suppliers to follow the same procedures. Grandin has since proclaimed that u.s.-based slaughterhouses are more advanced than European ones in terms of animal welfare.[30]

Other fast-food chains have developed policies to reflect public concern and perception. Chipotle's founder, Steve Ells, announced that the company's mission was to serve 'food with integrity'. The beef, chicken and pork used at Chipotle outlets comes from animals that have been treated humanely. Chipotle foods are free of trans fats, and the company uses organic and locally grown ingredients when possible. Its prices are higher, but its profits have been escalating while those of traditional American fast-food chains, such as McDonald's, have not.

Fast-food corporations have taken micro-steps in the right direction, but they need to take more responsibility for controlling the unsustainable harm caused by their meat suppliers and improve the nutritional content of the beef, pork and chicken that they serve. Harvey Blatt, author of *America's Food: What You Don't Know About What You Eat* (2011), offered an easier solution: 'Perhaps children at fast-food restaurants should be told by Ronald McDonald that hamburgers are ground up cows that were killed by a metal rod shot into their heads before their throats were slit by a machete so their blood could be drained.' He also suggested that children should be told that Willard Scott, who created Ronald McDonald, is now a vegetarian.[31]

7
LABOUR

At 6:30 am on 29 November 2012, about 100 workers from McDonald's, Burger King, Domino's, KFC, Taco Bell, Wendy's and Papa John's restaurants in New York City walked off the job. Along with a few allies, they marched down Madison Avenue, chanting, 'Hey, hey, what do you say? We demand fair pay!' Others engaged in sit-ins at fast-food restaurants or (safely) blockaded the entrances. The intention of the one-day 'flash strike' was not to shut down the restaurants for any length of time, but to draw the public's attention to the low pay and lack of union representation in fast-food restaurants. The strike was also intended to embarrass the fast-food industry, whose employees are among America's worst paid.

Similar one-day actions followed throughout the country, with thousands demonstrating outside fast-food chains in 200 American cities. Demonstrators carried signs proclaiming, 'No Justice, No Peace', 'Sí, Se Puede' (Yes We Can), 'Low Pay is Not OK', 'McDonald's Won't Listen', 'On Strike to Lift My Family Up', and 'Stick Together for $15 and Union Rights'. In one strike protesters blocked traffic on New York City's busiest streets. The police told them to leave; when 56 of the demonstrators refused to move, they were arrested. In other cities where such actions were held an estimated 500 people were arrested.

These strikes were organized by the Service Employees International Union (SEIU), one of America's largest unions, representing 1.9 million workers in healthcare, janitorial and other occupations. It started organizing fast-food chains in 2009. Since then, SEIU has spent an estimated $10 million on these efforts. Rather than trying to incite traditional long-term strikes, the SEIU decided on a different strategy – one-day wildcat strikes to publicize the plight of fast-food workers. The SEIU helped to organize groups in cities to organize and spearhead local strikes. This was a media-centric plan intended to gain high visibility for fast-food workers and embarrass their employers.

In addition to national strikes, labour organizers took their campaign to McDonald's corporate headquarters in Oak Brook, Illinois. In May 2014, during McDonald's annual shareholder meeting, fast-food workers and their allies picketed roads leading into the McDonald's complex. McDonald's directed most of its 3,200 headquarters employees to stay at home during the strike. More than 100 protesters, including Mary Kay Henry, the SEIU president, were arrested. The fast-food worker strikes have picked up steam. Scores of strikes and other labour actions have been held in cities around the world. On 15 April 2015 fast-food and other workers demonstrated in 236 American cities. Henry declared that 'It showed that if we come together things can change. There's momentum behind working people joining together to improve their lives – that's what this movement is about.'[1]

The fast-food industry is global, and workers in countries throughout the world face many of the same problems that challenge U.S. workers. American union organizers visited other countries to help organize workers and form a global fast-food employees' union. This groundwork paid off in May 2014, when fast-food workers engaged in strikes in 33 countries, including India, Brazil, the UK, Japan and the Philippines.

In the UK, where the current national minimum wage for workers over the age of 21 is £6.50 (about U.S.$10), rallies have been held outside fast-food outlets, and Labour MPs led a protest outside Parliament in 2014. The Bakers, Food and Allied Workers' Union (BFAWU) sought to increase the fast-food workers' hourly wage to £10. In 2014 it launched a campaign called 'Fast Food Rights', using the slogan 'Hungry for Justice'.

Background

The low wages paid to restaurant staff are one major reason for fast food's financial success. Most workers are part-timers who receive hourly wages without medical or other benefits. At most chains wages are set by area managers according to local laws and conditions. Managers are encouraged to keep labour costs down, and are rewarded with bonuses when they cut wages or eliminate employees. This sometimes leads to abuse, as understaffed operations force workers to increase their pace; sometimes they are required to work 'off the clock' if they want to keep their jobs (which saves on overtime). Fired employees have been informally blacklisted to prevent their being hired by other fast-food entities. These practices are against the law, but many employees, especially undocumented immigrants or others desperate for income, are too timid to challenge illegal practices; they're simply too fearful of being fired or deported.

Fast-food chains have been charged with violating pay and hour rules, but Subway, the fast-food chain with the largest number of outlets worldwide (more than 42,000), has the largest number of violations in America. According to the Department of Labor's Wage and Hour Division, more than 1,100 violations of pay and hour rules have been found in Subway franchises spanning the period from 2000 to 2013.[2]

While restaurants have always paid low salaries (and in some cases no salaries – just tips), the current fast-food model dates to decisions made by Dick and Mac McDonald, who, in 1940, opened the 'McDonald Brothers Burger Bar Drive-in'. It boasted twenty female carhops who took orders, delivered them to customers sitting in cars parked at the front, and then collected payment. After the Second World War the brothers had a hard time finding competent employees: the American economy was booming, and many men who had been in the services were attending college. The limited labour pool left the McDonalds desperate: they complained of their fry cooks and dishwashers drinking on the job, and were dissatisfied with the carhops, who were more interested in socializing with teenage boys than in selling burgers.

The McDonald brothers decided to tighten things up: they would reduce expenses and increase profits through improved efficiency. They developed an assembly-line system that divided the work into simple tasks that could be performed with a minimum of training. This meant that employees were essentially interchangeable and could easily be shifted from one task to another. The customer got a fast, reliable, cheap meal; in return for that service, the McDonald brothers expected them to stand in line, pick up their orders, eat quickly, clean up their own litter and then hit the road, making room for the next paying customer.

This model created a semi-militarized production system based on a workforce of teenage boys, who were responsible for simple, easily taught tasks: flipping burgers, wrapping them, pouring beverages, frying french fries or bagging orders. It was a first job for many of these youngsters, and they were willing to work for the minimum wage (managers could pay 'apprentices' under the age of eighteen even less than that). The workers received virtually no benefits – no paid holiday, healthcare or job protection. With no paid sick days, many went to work even when they were feeling ill. Still, the job taught them basic work skills, such as promptness, teamwork, obedience to supervisors and personal hygiene. The average employee worked for only a few months before quitting or being fired. High turnover has remained a consistent pattern. Employee turnover today averages about 75 per cent per year. These days, with a large pool of willing (not to say desperate) applicants for a minimum-wage job with no benefits, rapid employee turnover does not create hardship for restaurant managers.

The postwar growth of the American fast-food industry coincided with the coming of age of the baby boomers. It was enhanced when the industry broadened employment opportunities for women and minorities in the 1970s. Today the American fast-food industry employs a disproportionate number of women and minorities in high-speed, high-pressure, low-wage, dead-end jobs. Ironically the industry has benefited greatly from the women's movement: since housewives traditionally did the family's shopping and cooking, women's entry into the workforce increased demand for fast food as a cheap alternative to home cooking.[3]

For 60 years the fast-food industry has thrived by paying workers poorly and keeping unions at a distance. Trade unions have yet to succeed in organizing American fast-food workers. A major reason for this failure has been the industry's strenuous anti-union efforts. As Eric Schlosser notes in *Fast Food Nation* (2001), it has been almost impossible for unions to gain a foothold in the fast-food industry. The high staff turnover, the part-time nature of the job, the low economic status of staff and the decentralized way in which the chains set wages have made it difficult to organize workers. Fast-food chains have gone to extraordinary lengths to keep trade unions out. During the early 1970s McDonald's sent a so-called 'flying squad' of experienced managers and corporate executives to outlets where union activity was suspected. McDonald's employees in the San Francisco Bay area claimed that they were forced to take lie-detector tests so the chain could identify union sympathizers. McDonald's has reportedly squashed 'hundreds' of unionization drives.[4]

In the 1970s the Association of Community Organizers for Reform Now (ACORN), a collection of organizations that advocated for low-income families, launched a drive to organize fast-food workers in Detroit. It published a weekly newsletter, *Fast Food Worker*, as a way to organize employees at local Burger King and McDonald's outlets. On 29 February 1979 Burger King workers at one outlet voted by 25 to 23 for a union. The company challenged five ballots; a new election was held, and this time the proposed union was defeated. Organizing efforts at McDonald's outlets in Detroit also failed. McDonald's illegally fired employees believed to support the union and warned workers that they would lose benefits if they voted for union representation. In May 1980 McDonald's workers voted the union down.[5]

It's difficult to organize workers whose tasks are rote and interchangeable, making staff easily replaceable. If a strike were called, new workers could be slotted in within a short time. The Industrial Workers of the World (iww) launched a Starbucks Workers Union in 2004 that now has members at eight Starbucks locations in the United States. In July 2008 the iww launched a 'Global Day of Action' in response to Starbucks anti-union practices, and similar actions have taken place in more than twenty countries. Subsequently the iww tried to organize fast-food workers. They specifically targeted fast-food workers at Jimmy John's, a small sandwich chain in Minneapolis. The iww demands included free uniforms, paid sick days, extra pay for early morning hours, paid maternity and paternity leave, guaranteed hours, a short lunch break for shifts of six hours or more, health and dental insurance plans, and regular meetings with managers. In 2010 workers in the chain voted on whether to unionize. The vote was 87 in favour and 85 against, although the vc´ was declared invalid by the court. The organizers to⌐˙

company to court, claiming that the owners engaged in unfair labour practices, retaliated against a number of workers for organizing activity, and promised pay rises and holiday pay to those who would undermine the union's efforts. The court found in favour of the organizers. In 2011 the Jimmy John's staff was given a second opportunity to vote for union representation; they turned it down with a larger majority.

Automation

From the beginning, fast-food chains have tried to automate their operations to reduce the need for skilled workers. Automated kitchens are equipped with buzzers and flashing lights that tell employees what to do and when to do it. Computerized cash registers issue their own instructions. Hence new employees require little training, and their departure is not a great loss. Chains are currently experimenting with new automated systems, such as machines that can cook hundreds of hamburgers per hour and smartphone or computer ordering systems that have food ready for pickup when the customer arrives.

In selected cities fast-food chains such as Domino's, Papa John's, Burger King and McDonald's have turned to mobile devices for ordering delivery service. Other experimental systems permit customers to place their orders on a computer screen at the outlet and pay for them via credit card. At one McDonald's in Oak Brook, Illinois, customers can build their own hamburger by choosing from more than twenty ingredients on a touch screen. They then sit down and a server brings their hamburgers to their table. This speeds up the ordering process, improves accuracy and reduces labour costs. Customers don't have to wait in long queues and fast-food chains increase their profits. According to a report by NPD, a market research firm, online ordering has more than doubled from around $403 million in 2010 to $904 million by May 2015.

Minimum Wage

In the U.S. the federal minimum wage is currently $7.25 per hour (as of 2015). Although it has increased over the years, it has not kept pace with inflation. According to the Congressional Research Service, a non-partisan body of the U.S. Congress, the current minimum wage is worth less than three-quarters of its value in 1968. The decline in the value of the minimum wage relative to average wages is even greater, and this change illustrates the increasing financial inequality in America.

Some states and cities have a higher minimum wage, set by local government. Pay rates for specific employees are set by fast-food managers based on local labour conditions. Fast-food employees make a median wage of $8.69 per hour, which makes them the lowest-paid workers in America. Most employees are not allowed to work full-time, few have guaranteed working hours, and most cannot control their schedules owing to zero-hours contracts. Some suffer verbal abuse, racial or ethnic discrimination or sexual harassment. There is little chance of medical or other benefits and minimal opportunity for upward mobility.

Many workers claim that chains engage in 'wage theft'. This includes a wide range of illegal actions such as paying workers less than minimum wage; requiring them to work, without compensation, before or after their shift; requiring them to work overtime without being paid time-and-a-half, as required by law; forcing them to work through their breaks; and failing to reimburse their expenses. Between busy times workers have been required to remain at the fast-food outlet, but not work, and hence are not paid for those downtime hours. A survey of New York City fast-food workers reported that 89 per cent claimed some form of wage theft.[6] A 2008 study by the National Employment Law Project estimated that wage theft amounted to about 15 per cent of the fast-food workers' salaries.

This doesn't only happen in America. In Europe McDonald's has been charged with giving incorrect pay and classifying workers in lower pay grades, for example by defining them as 'apprentices'.[7] In 2014 a Burger King franchisee in Germany was charged with wage theft, failure to pay promised bonuses for working on holidays, and failure to give sick pay.[8] In 2007 Chinese labour officials in Guangdong Province charged KFC, McDonald's and Pizza Hut franchises with paying part-time workers 4 to 5 yuan (52 to 65 U.S. cents) per hour, about 30–40 per cent under the legal minimum wage.[9]

Americans working in the lower echelons of the fast-food industry do not make enough to cover their expenses or support their families. About 20 per cent of fast-food workers' families live below the poverty line. An estimated 52 per cent of fast-food workers receive public assistance,

much of it in the form of food aid.[10] About 87 per cent of
fast-food workers do not receive health benefits from their
employers. Other public assistance includes earned income
tax credits, Medicaid, the Children's Health Insurance
Program and Temporary Assistance for Needy Families.[11]
As a result American taxpayers pay an estimated $7 billion
per year to cover public assistance for fast-food workers.[12]
When all restaurant workers are included, American
taxpayers pay a total of $152.8 billion per year to cover
their public assistance.[13]

Fast-food chains hire new immigrants, particularly
Hispanics and Asians, with limited literacy or English
vocabulary. Undocumented immigrants are often willing
to work off the books, and rarely complain to authorities of
abuse. Recognizing the importance of their undocumented
workers, chains and franchises have strongly supported
national immigration reform efforts. Chains also hire
disabled people, whose wages are frequently subsidized
by government programmes.

The fast-food industry is one of the nation's largest
employers of minimum- and low-wage workers. It pays
minimum wages to a higher percentage of workers than any
other u.s. industry. It would take a full-time fast-food worker
on $8.69 an hour about four months to earn what Don
Thompson, the former ceo of McDonald's, made in an hour:
about $9,247 with benefits.[14] Perhaps some could support
this disparity if McDonald's was generating vast profits for its
shareholders, but in fact company sales have been declining
while other chains have been surging ahead. Slumping sales
were why Thompson was ousted as ceo in 2015.

Despite this wide disparity in salaries, the National Restaurant Association, which represents American restaurants including fast-food chains, has lobbied against increases in minimum wage at city, state and national levels. They insist that fast-food jobs are ideal first jobs, perfect for anyone who wants to work part-time. Historically many employees were teenagers living at home. Today the average age of workers has increased to 29.[15] More than 25 per cent are parents, raising at least one child, and 68 per cent of the fast-food workforce are the main wage earners for their families: these are not people who can live on an entry-level wage.[16]

Fast-food chains reward managers who keep labour costs low. For example, they have paid their managers bonuses based on the reduction of labour costs. This has sometimes led to abuse, such as employees working off the books. Industry representatives claim that their jobs are largely for unskilled workers who can easily be replaced. They have also complained that if wages were increased, sales would decline and franchises would lose out on profits. As prices – and profits – have regularly increased over the decades, this is a hollow argument.

Where fast-food strikes have worked is in urging local and state governments to increase the minimum wage: Massachusetts increased its minimum wage to $11 an hour. In California, Oakland has raised its minimum wage to $12.25; Berkeley to $12.53. Seattle and San Francisco city councils have approved city minimum wages that will increase to $15 over the next few years. In 2015 the International Franchise Association, which represents the fast-food industry, challenged the $15 minimum wage in Seattle, claiming that it was unconstitutional, and promptly lost in court. Other cities and a few states are considering increasing minimum wages. In 2015 Los Angeles approved a raise to $15 by 2020 and New York State approved a graduated pay rise to $15 for all 200,000 fast-food workers in the state.

Nigel Travis, the chief executive of Dunkin' Donuts, said that a $15 minimum wage for fast-food workers was 'absolutely outrageous'. Travis made no such comment when his own pay was increased from $4.3 million in 2013 to $10.2 million in 2014.

At the federal level, President Obama has called on Congress to increase the minimum wage to $9 an hour and Congressional Democrats introduced the Fair Minimum Wage Act of 2013, which had no chance of passing. In 2015 Obama upped his request, calling for the federal minimum wage to increase to $10.10 an hour and for future minimum wage hikes to be indexed to the cost of living. He also urged employers to offer sick leave and other benefits. In February 2015 Obama challenged Congressmen to try living on $15,000 a year, and again urged them to raise the minimum wage. To date, no Congressional action has been taken. Fast-food workers continue to eke out a living, while the fast-food industry continues to generate handsome profits for corporate leaders, stockholders and franchisers.

Franchisees and Franchisers

Most American fast-food outlets are owned and operated by local and regional franchisees, who hire, discipline and fire staff, set wages and create schedules for workers. Franchisees buy the rights to a fast-food corporation's name, national advertising, products, equipment and systems of operation. For these and other services, franchisees send a share of their profits to the national corporation.

A major challenge to fast-food unionization has been an old ruling by the National Labor Relations Board (NLRB), an independent agency of the federal government that investigates and resolves unfair labour practices. During the 1980s, the NLRB ruled that franchisers were not liable for the employment practices of their franchisees, as the franchiser was not directly responsible for hiring and firing employees. This covered a very broad swathe of the industry, because national fast-food corporations, such as McDonald's USA, Burger King and Yum! Brands, control most of the fast-food outlets in the United States. Workers could sue only their immediate employer, the franchisee – not the larger corporate entity. Labour organizers had to concentrate their efforts on thousands of individual franchises rather than on a single entity. In the unlikely event that such an organizing effort succeeded at a franchise, the national corporation could change franchisees, thus invalidating the existing union and forcing organizers to start all over again. The Service Employees International Union and the National Employment Law Project, a worker advocacy group, maintain that fast-food chains indirectly control their franchisees' workers through rules, restrictions and equipment.

In 2014 the NLRB overturned the ruling that franchisers were not responsible for the welfare of franchise employees. In May 2014 the Fast Food Workers Committee in New York specifically charged that the local McDonald's franchisee had fired nine workers because of their union organizing activities from November 2012 to April 2014. Other union organizers declared that McDonald's had cut their hours, threatened to fire them or disciplined them in other ways. In December 2014 the NLRB brought 78 charges against McDonald's franchisees and McDonald's USA, as joint employers, for violating federal labour law relating to the fast-food strikes during the previous two years. The charges include 'discriminatory discipline, reductions in hours, discharges, and other coercive conduct directed at employees in response to union and protected concerted activity, including threats, surveillance, interrogations, promises of benefit, and overboard restrictions on communicating with union representatives or with other employees about unions and the employees' terms and conditions of employment'. The NLRB is considering bringing charges against other fast-food corporations for similar activities.[17] If the 30-year-old NLRB ruling is reversed, making national chains accountable as joint employers, it will be a big win for labour organizers in the fast-food industry.

In a 2014 Labor Day speech, President Obama spoke in support of the fast-food strikes. He reminded his audience, 'All across the country right now there's a national movement going on made up of fast-food workers organizing to lift wages so they can provide for their families with pride and dignity.'[18]

Suppliers

American fast-food outlets are the endpoints of long food chains: their beef can be raised in Kansas or California; their iceberg lettuce in Arizona; their poultry in North Carolina; their potatoes in Idaho; and their tomatoes in Florida. While fast-food chains may be judged to have no *direct* authority over the wages or working conditions of their suppliers, they certainly have an indirect responsibility.

Until the 1960s America's meatpacking industry was unionized and fairly safe, and it provided relatively highly paid jobs. When fast-food chains became major purchasers of meat, corporate headquarters negotiated contracts with potential suppliers. Large fast-food chains used their purchasing power to negotiate among suppliers for the lowest price. Lower prices resulted in a sharp drop in wages, less training for employees and slacker safety requirements. Employees were forced to speed up slaughtering and butchering. Eric Schlosser reported that 'In the old Chicago packinghouses teams of workers disassembled about fifty cattle an hour and performed a variety of tasks throughout the day. In modern American slaughterhouses the line speeds can approach four hundred cattle an hour, and the new division of labor requires workers to perform the same task again and again.'[19] In addition to the dangers for workers, the tremendous increase in the amount of product being handled caused meat and poultry to become more susceptible to the introduction of pathogens, such as *Salmonella* and *E. coli* O157:H7.

One place where unions have partly succeeded is in the tomato fields of Florida. In 1996 the migrant workers formed the Coalition of Immokalee Workers (CIW), which attempted to raise wages and improve working and living conditions for the tomato pickers. They were opposed by the Florida Tomato Growers Exchange, an industry lobby group whose members control 90 per cent of the winter tomato crop. To gain visibility for the plight of the workers, in 2001 the CIW called for a national boycott of Taco Bell, one of the largest buyers of winter tomatoes. College, high-school and religious groups, including the National Council of Churches, joined the boycott. In 2005 Taco Bell agreed to pay a penny more per pound for its tomatoes, provided that the money went to improving the working and living conditions of the workers.

During the next five years, other major fast-food companies, including Yum! Brands (owner of Pizza Hut, Taco Bell and KFC), McDonald's, Burger King and Subway, agreed to pay one cent (or more) extra per pound, but the Florida tomato growers refused to participate. In November 2010 the growers finally agreed in principle to a 'Fair Food Code of Conduct'. Funds generated by this agreement will go towards increasing workers' annual pay to an estimated $17,000. Farm labourers will be educated about their rights and how to report violations, including sexual harassment of women workers, and there will be a third-party system to help resolve disputes. Despite some success, conditions for farm workers in the Florida tomato fields remain grim, as documented in Barry Estabrook's book *Tomatoland* (2011) and Kanti Rawal's film *Food Chains* (2015), produced by Eric Schlosser and Eva Longoria.

Crimes and Injuries

In addition to suffering poor working conditions, fast-food workers have been the victims of serious crimes. In the 1920s White Castle, the first fast-food chain, built its outlets in inner cities near transportation hubs; most of its customers were workers from nearby industries. To reach night-shift workers, outlets were generally open late at night. As inner cities deteriorated during the 1950s, crime, violence, racial tension and vagrancy increasingly became problems for inner-city fast-food chains. Chains invested heavily in security measures and instituted earlier closing times at vulnerable outlets, but problems persisted.

After the Second World War many chains set their sights on the suburbs in part to avoid these urban problems. When the suburbs became saturated with fast-food outlets, chains refocused on inner cities, and found these outlets highly profitable. Wherever they are found, fast-food outlets remain targets for crime, particularly robberies. They typically open early in the morning and stay open late (many chains feature 'after-midnight' menus), making them attractive to robbers. They do most of their business in cash, which means that by late evening many outlets have thousands of dollars on their premises. In addition, many fast-food restaurants are near off-ramps, and drive-through windows permit fast getaways. Employees who deliver fast food, such as pizza, to homes face their own perils. In the 1990s in the u.s. four to five fast-food workers were killed every month while at work, usually during the course of a robbery. In 1998 more restaurant workers than policemen were murdered on the job in America.

These appalling numbers have declined since then, but robberies have increased, largely because alternative targets, such as gas stations, now largely operate on credit cards, reducing the amount of cash on hand. But the U.S. Bureau of Labor reports that even when compared with full-service restaurants, the rate of assaults at 'limited service' restaurants outlets is twice as high.

Fast-food chains target specific demographics that generate high traffic and profits, and fail to properly prepare for the increased risk of crime that may accompany such choices. When the Occupational Safety and Health Administration (OSHA), the American federal agency responsible for workers' safety, proposed guidelines for preventing violence at restaurants that do business at night, restaurateurs opposed those guidelines. They did not want the OSHA to impose fines or compel security measures, and companies were afraid that employees would use the guidelines to bring lawsuits against chains where violence occurred.

Faced with lawsuits and negative publicity, fast-food chains have reduced violence by installing new security measures, such as highly visible CCTV cameras inside and outside outlets, multiple panic buttons, drop and time-delay safes, burglar alarms and better lighting. Outlets now accept credit cards, which limits the amount of in-store cash. Other chains have limited their hours for indoor dining and installed bullet-resistant glazing on drive-through windows. Despite these changes, fast-food stores remain major targets for robberies, and workers on late-night shifts remain particularly vulnerable.

Fast-food chain employees are sometimes themselves responsible for crimes – especially inside theft. Managers often fail to screen potential employees adequately and may not conduct even basic criminal background checks. As a result, no other industry is robbed so frequently by its own employees. The combination of low pay, high turnover, no background checks and ample cash has made fast-food outlets ideal for employee theft. Disgruntled and discharged employees have also been known to target outlet employees with violent behaviour.

Crime is one cause of injury at fast-food outlets, but health and safety deficiencies hurt many more workers. An estimated 14,000 fast-food staffers end up in hospital emergency rooms every year owing to on-the-job injuries, according to a report by the National Institute for Occupational Safety and Health. The most common causes are burns, lacerations and other injuries related to cooking, and sprains, strains and contusions from falls, often caused by wet or greasy floors. In a recent survey of fast-food workers, most claimed that they had suffered injuries while working at fast-food chains. In March 2015, 28 workers filed complaints against McDonald's alleging that understaffing and pressure from managers to work faster led to on-the-job burns and falls.[20]

Higher Wages and Zero Hours

Workers in other countries have also tried to unionize with mixed results. In 1998 the McDonald's Workers Resistance in Glasgow launched a campaign for wage increases and other work-related changes. More recently, the Scottish Trades Union Congress (STUC) organized a campaign in Scotland seeking an initial increase to £7.85 and eventually to £10 per

hour.[21] They are also arguing for an end to zero-hours contracts, a system where employers have the discretion to alter
the employee's weekly working hours from full-time to zero.
Employees have no guaranteed work from week to week.
Concerns with zero-hours contracts are present in other
countries, such as New Zealand, where many workers are
members of Unite Union. Thanks to union pressure, Burger
King, Wendy's and McDonald's have all agreed to end zero-
hours contracts in New Zealand.[22] In Germany workers at
McDonald's outlets have been fired for showing sympathy
towards unions, reported Siegfried Pater in *Zum Beispiel
McDonald's* (2000).[23] Compared with North American
and European fast-food operations, working conditions and
wages are often much worse in the rapidly growing fast-food
industry in low-income countries.

There are a few places where fast-food workers do
not suffer from low pay, a lack of benefits and deplorable
working conditions. In Denmark the United Federation of
Danish Workers ('3F') negotiated contracts with fast-food
chains in mid-2000. Today, Danish fast-food workers earn
a minimum of 115 kroner ($19.35, £12.35) per hour – about
two-and-a-half times what their American counterparts
are paid. The Danish workers enjoy paid holiday, maternity
and paternity leave, pension plans and paid overtime, and
their schedules are set four weeks in advance. (Their medical
expenses are covered by governmental programmes.) As
the *New York Times* reported, 'If McDonald's can afford to
pay that in Denmark they should be able to pay more everywhere. It is the same work, but a huge difference in pay.'[24]
Fast-food workers in the other Scandinavian countries have

made similar progress. The Nordisk Union HRTC represents fast-food workers in Sweden, Norway, Denmark, Finland and Iceland.

Fast-food companies also have contracts with unions in other European countries and Australia and New Zealand. Worker councils have been set up in many countries, although fast-food corporations have engaged in tactics to prevent them from so doing, according to Tony Royle, author of *Working for McDonald's in Europe: The Unequal Struggle?* (2001). Where fast-food workers have collective bargaining agreements, workers' pay has increased.[25] Unionized fast-food operations have better benefits as well. Full-time workers at McDonald's in the Netherlands and Germany who work for just three weeks are entitled to two days of paid holiday and other benefits.[26] Fast-food franchises in countries with union representation still generate healthy profits for their owners – although not as substantial as in the U.S. In New Zealand, where a Big Mac costs about $4.49, full-time union workers make U.S. $12.35 per hour.[27]

Even in the U.S., higher wages are paid by some fast-food chains, such as In-N-Out Burger, a California-based regional chain, where the average hourly pay for a worker is $12. In Shake Shack, a New York-based chain, workers average $10.70 per hour – well above the fast-food industry's median hourly wage of $8.69. For full-time employees, Shake Shack also covers 70 per cent of healthcare premiums (including dental and vision), matches employee contributions to 401(k) pension funds and offers paid leave.

On 1 April 2015 McDonald's announced a 10 per cent pay rise in all corporate-owned stores in the United States. This did not include franchises, which make up 90 per cent of McDonald's restaurants. Many franchisees were not happy with this public relations move as they were now under public pressure to raise their salaries. Mary Kay Henry, president of the Service Employees International Union, wasn't happy either: 'McDonald's was forced to pay up, but it's not nearly enough.'[28] McDonald's sweetened the pot with an offer to cover a portion of college tuition costs for employees who work at least twenty hours per week and for managers in all u.s. outlets, including franchises. Starbucks followed McDonald's' lead and offered its employees similar tuition assistance.[29]

Paying partial college tuition is a nice perk for a few workers and a nice public relations ploy for fast-food companies, but it doesn't buy food for the industry's under-paid workers or their families. The fast-food industry has a long way to go before it meets its responsibilities to its employees.

8
THE FUTURE

The fast-food industry is a global goliath that is expanding in virtually every corner of the world. For better and for worse, fast food is the most influential culinary trend of our time and affects hundreds of millions of people every day. Access to reasonably tasty food with speed, economy, convenience and anonymity appeals to customers of different nationalities, ethnicities, religions, ages, genders, classes, financial status and culinary traditions. Anchored by huge multinational corporations, the industry also offers opportunities for indigenous startups in countries worldwide to embark on their own fast-food ventures. Chains provide jobs (albeit unskilled, low-paying ones) for millions of workers, very few of whom rise through the ranks into management positions.

During its first half-century of largely unfettered growth, the industry has had negative effects on the environment, exposed its customers to health risks, degraded the diets of children and underpaid its workers. Indirectly, through its suppliers, it has supported factory farming and condoned dangerous working conditions from field to processing plant. The fast-food industry has undersold indigenous food purveyors, contributed to the loss of local and regional diversity and promoted culinary homogenization around the world.

When called to account for this damage, fast-food chains have made changes – occasionally substantial, but more often token – in their operations. More commonly, the industry has denied responsibility, blamed customers, castigated suppliers, opposed regulations and initiatives, funded sympathetic political candidates and organizations, sued opponents, blocked unionization and launched media blitzes in the face of negative publicity.

Few positive steps taken by fast-food chains have satisfied their critics, and the controversies that engulf the industry will not be resolved any time soon. Despite the growing awareness of its problems, fast food is here to stay. The good news is that the future of the industry is in the hands of its customers.

It is not in the industry's interest to harm or appear to harm its customers, yet chains serve outsized, highly calorific portions of foods that are high in fat, saturated fat and sodium. The damage already done to the health of fast-food consumers will have long-lasting repercussions. While some localities have imposed regulations and restrictions on fast-food outlets – zoning, nutritional labelling, elimination of toys in kids' meals and bans on marketing directly to children – the fast-food industry can do much more to solve the health problems it has created: truly healthful options, especially for children's meals, can be added to the menu. Recipes can be reformulated to reduce fat, sugar and sodium. In fact research suggests that the calories in fast-food meals could be trimmed by as much as 30 per cent without consumers even being aware of the changes. Likewise, sodium could be reduced over time without the change being noticeable. Portion sizes could be trimmed, and high-fibre ingredients could replace those that are more calorie-dense. Innovations like these could make a world of difference, especially for people who eat fast food on a regular basis.

Some fast-food chains have undertaken to limit their use of non-renewable energy and eliminate unrecyclable waste. This can improve the bottom line, and such 'green' projects also bring the companies positive publicity. But they need to do more than showcase a few model outlets and institute energy-saving programmes at corporate headquarters. Fast-food chains could require franchisees to make energy-saving structural changes and put in place greener operating procedures and recycling programmes. Everybody wins when chains improve energy efficiency in their operations.

Fast-food companies must improve and publicize the requirements they place on their suppliers. If suppliers do not comply with these strictures, they stand to lose business and sacrifice profits. If fast-food chains are unwilling to pursue constant surveillance of their suppliers, then nonprofit organizations should be brought in to serve as watchdogs. This is being done in some countries, and there is no reason why it should not become universal.

No fast-food chain should market its products to children and adolescents; neither should these companies promote or sell their products directly or indirectly through schools. Companies have pledged to suspend television advertising, but many have broken their promise, so governments must step in to block fast-food commercials on children's television programmes and other programmes airing before 9 pm. This will not spell the end of the fast-food industry: in countries that have banned all television advertising aimed at children, fast-food chains continue to thrive. New media pose new problems, and ways must be found to limit fast-food advertising through 'advergames', social media and apps. Fast-food chains should not dangle free toys in front of children in order to sell kids' meals. On the contrary, the chains need to create more healthful children's meals and find constructive ways to make them appealing to kids.

Today four fast-food corporations – Burger King, McDonald's, Yum! Brands (which manages KFC, Pizza Hut and Taco Bell) and Subway – employ about 4.5 million people worldwide and operate 162,000 restaurants. McDonald's alone hires 1 million new workers every year, more than any other American business. Decades ago, when most fast-food workers were teenagers looking for pocket money, the minimum wage was acceptable, but today's workers are adults, many of them supporting families. They must be paid a decent living wage. Fast-food companies protest that increased wages will mean higher prices, lower profits and fewer customers, resulting in fewer employment opportunities for those in need. This is not likely to be an accurate projection. Wages total about 26 per cent of total costs for fast-food chains; doubling the wages of the lowest-paid workers would increase costs by about 20 per cent. If wage increases were implemented incrementally over time, and prices were raised gradually as well, most customers wouldn't even notice, and fast-food chains would still be more affordable than full-service restaurants.

The growth of the fast-food industry will likely continue and accelerate, particularly in the developing world. Despite the fears of those who cherish traditional foodways, it is unlikely that fast food will obliterate venerable local cuisines, which will continue to thrive in homes and in full-service restaurants. However, unless governments promote (and customers demand) more healthful offerings, the fast-food industry will continue to serve up dishes that are high in calories, fat and salt. Providing affordable, accessible meals for busy individuals and families is a credit-worthy endeavour, so long as the food is wholesome and nourishing and the operation doesn't harm its customers, its workers or the environment. Surely this can be accomplished by companies with the size and clout of McDonald's, Burger King, Subway and Yum! Brands.

Fast-food-chain executives are not inherently bad, but like their counterparts in the tobacco companies before them, they are fully aware of the long-term ill-effects that their foods and beverages have on their frequent customers. Their justification is that they sell what customers want to buy. They fail to mention that their 50-year marketing campaigns, especially those aimed at children and adolescents, have created many of the wants that their customers now have. Chains will continue to advertise and sell menu items high in calories, sugar, fat and salt for as long as customers continue to order them. Companies will make the minimum changes necessary to avoid bad publicity, and will spend millions to prevent the passage of laws and policies that make it more difficult for them to turn a profit.

Ultimately customers are responsible for what they – and their children – eat. Likewise citizens are responsible for the actions that they take – or fail to take – in political and policy arenas to improve fast food's nutritional qualities, decrease its environmental harm, pay its workers a living wage and stop it being marketed to children and adolescents.

REFERENCES

1 THE BEGINNING

1 Karen S. Hamrick and Abigail M. Okrent, *The Role of Time in Fast-food Behavior in the United States*, u.s. Department of Agriculture, www.ers.usda.gov, November 2014.
2 Harvey Blatt, *America's Food: What You Don't Know About What You Eat* (Boston, MA, 2011), p. 113.
3 Kathryn M. Sharpe and Richard Staelin, 'Consumption Effects of Bundling: Consumer Perceptions, Firm Actions, and Public Policy Implications', *Journal of Public Policy and Marketing* (Fall 2010), www.archive.ama.org.
4 Martin B. Schmidt, 'Supertax Me', *New York Times*, www.nytimes. com, 19 October 2006.
5 'Technomic's Top 150 Fast-casual Chain Restaurant Report', www.technomic.com, 8 May 2014.
6 Maggie McGrath, 'How Millennials Will Dictate the Future of Fast Food', *Forbes*, www.forbes.com, 18 April 2014.
7 C. D. Fryar and R. B. Ervin, 'Caloric Intake from Fast Food among Adults: United States, 2007–2010', *NCHS Data Brief*, no. 114, National Center for Health Statistics, www.cdc.gov, 21 February 2013.
8 Brian Sozzi, 'Huge Fast Food Names are Quietly Testing Upscale Versions of Themselves', The Street, www.thestreet.com, 14 April 2015.

2 GLOBALIZATION

1 Quoted in Mary Davis Suro, 'Romans Protest McDonald's', *New York Times*, www.nytimes.com, 5 May 1986.
2 Philip B. Dwoskin, 'Foreign and Domestic Prospects for the u.s. Fast Food Franchise Industry', *Agricultural Economic*

Report No. 358 (USDA Economic Research Service, 1976), pp. 2, 7.

3 Agnes Stevenson, 'Britain Is Fast Food Capital of Europe; Ninety per cent of Parents Take Children to Burger Bars Despite Fears over Their Nutritional Value', *The Herald*, www.highbeam.com, 19 April 2002.

4 McDonald's UK, www.mcdonalds.co.uk, accessed 30 April 2015.

5 Takeaways in the UK include purchases at Chinese, Indian and other ethnic restaurants; these are typically family-owned and are not outlets of large chains. While takeaways undoubtedly contribute many of the same problems, such as obesity and environmental degradation, as do fast-food chains, they are not the focus of this book.

6 'Fast Food Britain Spends £29.4 Billion on Takeaways Every Year', VoucherCodes.co.uk, www.vouchercodes.co.uk, accessed 30 April 2015.

7 Henry Samuel, 'Fast Food Overtakes Traditional Cuisine in France for the First Time', *Daily Telegraph*, www.telegraph.co.uk, 28 February 2013.

8 Jim Hightower, *Eat your Heart Out: Food Profiteering in America* (New York, 1975), p. 237. No one paid much attention to the concept of McDonaldization in the 1970s, but it was adopted by the Slow Food Movement in 1986. The term 'McDonaldization' emerged in the academic community in the 1990s, when the sociologist George Ritzer published *The McDonaldization of Society: An Investigation into the Changing Character of Contemporary Social Life* (Thousand Oaks, CA, 1993), and also has since been applied to a variety of non-food areas.

9 Jessica Wohl, 'Fast-food Chain Restaurants Continue to Dominate, Data Show', *Chicago Tribune*, www.chicagotribune.com, 2 March 2015.

10 USDA Economic Research Service, 'Ag and Food Statistics: Charting the Essentials', www.ers.usda.gov, September 2014.

11 George Ritzer, *The Globalization of Nothing 2* (Thousand Oaks, CA, 2007), pp. 155–6.

12 Benjamin R. Barber, *Jihad vs. McWorld: How Globalism and Tribalism Are Reshaping the World* (New York, 1996).

13 José Bové and François Dufour, *The World Is Not for Sale: Farmers Against Junk Food* (New York, 2001), p. 53; Elaine

Ganley, 'Radical French Farmer Found Guilty of Vandalizing McDonald's Restaurant', ABC News, www.abcnews.go.com, accessed 30 April 2015.

14 Rory Carroll, 'Protesters Try to Halt Rise of Fast-food Giant in Italy', *The Guardian*, www.theguardian.com, 17 October 2000.

15 Tony Royle, *Working for McDonald's in Europe: The Unequal Struggle?* (New York, 2001), p. 19.

16 Raja Abdulrahim, 'KFC Gets a Bad Rap in Egypt', *Los Angeles Times*, www.articles.latimes.com, 7 February 2011.

17 Tom Parfitt, 'Vladimir Putin "Backs Russian Fast-food Rival to McDonald's"', *The Telegraph*, www.telegraph.co.uk, 9 April 2015.

18 Yungxiang Yan, 'Of Hamburger and Social Space: Consuming McDonald's in Beijing', in *Food and Culture: A Reader*, ed. Carole Counihan and Penny Van Esterik, 3rd edn (New York and London, 2012), p. 451.

19 Per Pinstrup-Andersen and Fuzhi Cheng, eds, *Case Studies in Food Policy for Developing Countries* (Ithaca, NY, 2009), p. 151.

20 'Fast-food Restaurants in China: Market Research Report', IBIS World, www.ibisworld.com, September 2014.

21 Restaurant Brands International, www.timhortons.com, accessed 1 May 2015.

22 Timothy J. Richards and Luis Padilla, 'Promotion and Fast Food Demand', *American Journal of Agricultural Economics*, XCI/1 (February 2009), p. 169.

23 A. O. Olutayo and O. Akanle, 'Fast Food in Ibadan: An Emerging Consumption Pattern', *Africa: Journal of the International African Institute*, LXXIX/2 (2009), pp. 207–27.

3 HEALTH

1 American Heart Association, 'Understanding Childhood Obesity, Statistical Sourcebook', www.heart.org, accessed 1 May 2015.

2 Agricultural Research Service, U.S. Department of Agriculture, 'National Nutrient Database for Standard Reference', www.ndb.nal.usda.gov, accessed 1 May 2015.

3 B. Lorson, H. Melgar-Quinonez and C. Taylor, 'Correlates of Fruit and Vegetable Intake in U.S. Children', *Journal of the American Dietetic Association*, CIX (2009), pp. 474–8.

4 Michael F. Jacobson, *Liquid Candy: How Soft Drinks are Harming Americans' Health*, 2nd edn, Center for Science in the Public Interest (Washington, DC, 2005).

5 Brian Elbel et al., 'Potential Effect of the New York City Policy Regarding Sugared Beverages', *New England Journal of Medicine*, CCCLXVII (August 2012), pp. 680–81.

6 Rick Noack, 'The French War on American-style Free Soda Refills', *Washington Post*, www.washingtonpost.com, 16 September 2014.

7 U.S. Department of Agriculture et al., 'Dietary Guidelines for Americans', www.health.gov, December 2010.

8 Brian Wansink, James E. Painter and Jill North, 'Bottomless Bowls: Why Visual Cues of Portion Size May Influence Intake', *Obesity Research*, XIII (2005), pp. 93–100.

9 David A. Kessler, *The End of Overeating: Taking Control of the Insatiable American Appetite* (Emmaus, PA, 2009), pp. 157–62.

10 Spurlock followed the film with two books: *Don't Eat this Book: Fast Food and the Supersizing of America* (2005) and *Supersized: Strange Tales from a Fast-food Culture* (2011).

11 Mariel M. Finucane, 'National, Regional, and Global Trends in Body-mass Index since 1980: Systematic Analysis of Health Examination Surveys and Epidemiological Studies with 960 Country-years and 9.1 Million Participants', *The Lancet*, www.thelancet.com, 4 February 2011.

12 'Obesity and Overweight', World Health Organization, www.who.int, 20 January 2015.

13 Office of the Surgeon General, *The Surgeon General's Call to Action to Prevent and Decrease Overweight and Obesity*, www.ncbi.nlm.nih.gov (2001).

14 Christine Gorman, 'Health: How to Eat Smarter', *Time*, www.time.com, 20 October 2003; H. M. Niemeier et al., 'Fast Food Consumption and Breakfast Skipping: Predictors of Weight Gain from Adolescence to Adulthood in a Nationally Representative Sample', *Journal of Adolescent Health*, XXXIX/6 (December 2006), pp. 842–9; S. Bowman and B. Vineyard, 'Fast Food Consumption of U.S. Adults: Impact on Energy and Nutrient Intakes and Overweight Status', *Journal of the American College of Nutrition*, XXIII/2 (2004), pp. 163–8; J. A. Satia et al., 'Eating at Fast-food Restaurants Is Associated with Dietary Intake, Demographic,

Psychosocial and Behavioural Factors among African Americans in North Carolina', *Public Health Nutrition*, vii/8 (December 2004), pp. 1089–96.

15 M. A. Pereira et al., 'Fast-food Habits, Weight Gain, and Insulin Resistance (the Cardia Study): 15-year Prospective Analysis', *The Lancet*, ccclxv (1 January 2005), pp. 36–42.

16 Roberto De Vogli, Anne Kouvonen and David Gimeno, 'The Influence of Market Deregulation on Fast Food Consumption and Body Mass Index: A Cross-national Time Series Analysis', *Bulletin of the World Health Organization*, www.who.int, 24 September 2013.

17 C. D. Fryar and R. B. Ervin, 'Caloric Intake from Fast Food among Adults: United States, 2007–2010', *nchs Data Brief*, no 114, National Center for Health Statistics, www.cdc.gov, February 2013; Catherine Winters, 'Fast-food Consumption Slows Down', LiveScience, www.livescience.com, 22 February 2013.

18 S. E. Fleischhacker et al., 'A Systematic Review of Fast Food Access Studies', *Obesity Review*, xii/5 (2011), pp. e460–e471.

19 David A. Alter and Karen Eny, 'The Relationship Between the Supply of Fast-food Chains and Cardiovascular Outcomes', *Canadian Journal of Public Health/Revue canadienne de santé publique*, xcix/3 (May–June 2005), pp. 173–7; Thomas Burgoine et al., 'Associations Between Exposure to Takeaway Food Outlets, Takeaway Food Consumption, and Body Weight in Cambridgeshire, uk: Population Based, Cross Sectional Study', *British Medical Journal*, www.bmj.com, March 2014.

20 Janne Boone-Heinonen et al., 'Fast Food Restaurants and Food Stores; Longitudinal Associations with Diet in Young to Middle-aged Adults: The cardia Study', *Archives of Internal Medicine*, clxxi/13 (2011), pp. 1162–70.

21 Alicia Chang, 'Study: Limit on Fast-food Outlets in South Los Angeles Failed to Reduce Obesity, Improve Diets', *u.s. News and World Report*, www.usnews.com, 19 March 2015.

22 Dana Dabelea et al., 'Prevalence of Type 1 and Type 2 Diabetes Among Children and Adolescents from 2001 to 2009', *Journal of the American Medical Association*, cccxi/17 (7 May 2014), pp. 1778–86.

23 Kiyah J. Duffey et al., 'Regular Consumption from Fast Food Establishments Relative to Other Restaurants is Differentially

Associated with Metabolic Outcomes in Young Adults', *Journal of Nutrition* (November 2009), www.ncbi.nlm.nih.gov.

24 Pereira et al., 'Fast-food Habits, Weight Gain, and Insulin Resistance', pp. 36–42.

25 M. T. Ta et al., 'Identification of Undiagnosed Type 2 Diabetes by Systolic Blood Pressure and Waist-to-hip Ratio', *Diabetologia*, LIII (October 2010), pp. 2139–46.

26 Andrew O. Odegaard et al., 'Epidemiology and Prevention: Western-style Fast Food Intake and Cardiometabolic Risk in an Eastern Country', *Circulation*, 126 (July 2012), pp. 182–8.

27 Food Safety and Inspection Service, 'Nationwide Federal Plant Raw Ground Beef Microbiological Survey August 1993–March 1994', U.S. Department of Agriculture, www.fsis.usda.gov, April 1996.

28 Harvey Blatt, *America's Food: What You Don't Know About What You Eat* (Boston, MA, 2011), p. 203.

29 James Andrews, 'Analysis: "Restaurant A" Revealed to Be Taco Bell', *Food Safety News*, www.foodsafetynews.com, 2 February 2012.

30 Alice Park, 'Which Will Make You Sicker: Four Star v. Fast Food', *Time*, www.time.com, 24 April 2014.

31 Scripps Research Institute, 'News & Views', www.scripps.edu, 6 February 2012.

32 Michael Moss, *Salt Sugar Fat: How the Food Giants Hooked Us* (New York, 2013), p. 10.

33 Dana M. Small and Ralph J. DiLeone, eds, 'Food Addiction?', *Biological Psychiatry*, LXXIII/9 (1 May 2013), pp. A1–A10, E15–E32, 797–930.

34 Nicole M. Avena et al., 'Evidence for Sugar Addiction: Behavioral and Neurochemical Effects of Intermittent, Excessive Sugar Intake', *Neuroscience and Biobehavioral Reviews*, XXXII/1 (2008), pp. 20–39.

35 Consensus Action on Salt and Health, 'New Survey Names and Shames UK's "Saltiest" Family-friendly Eateries and Warns of a New Generation of "Salt Addicts"', www.actiononsalt.org.uk, 12 March 2015; quotation in Ben Spencer, 'Restaurant Children's Meals with Over a Day's Worth of Salt', *Daily Mail*, www.dailymail.co.uk, 15 March 2015.

36 Ashley N. Gearhardt, William R. Corbin and Kelly D. Brownell, 'Preliminary Validation of the Yale Food Addiction Scale', *Appetite*, LII/2 (2009), pp. 430–36.

37 Matthew Boyle, 'Can You Really Make Fast Food Healthy?',
    Fortune Magazine, www.fortune.com, 9 August 2004; Leslie
    Patton, 'McDonald's Pushing Meat as Salads Fail to Lure Diners',
    Bloomberg, www.bloomberg.com, 29 May 2013.
38 Lorien E. Urban et al., 'Temporal Trends in Fast-food Restaurant
    Energy, Sodium, Saturated Fat, and Trans Fat Content, United
    States, 1996–2013', *Preventing Chronic Disease*, www.cdc.gov,
    31 December 2014.
39 Eric A. Finkelstein et al., 'Mandatory Menu Labeling
    in One Fast-food Chain in King County, Washington',
    American Journal for Preventive Medicine, XL (February 2011),
    pp. 122–7; Brian Elbel, Rogan Kersh, Victoria L. Brescoll and
    L. Beth Dixon, 'Calorie Labeling and Food Choices: A First
    Look at the Effects on Low-income People in New York City',
    Health Affairs, XXVIII/6 (2009), pp. w1110–w1121; Nicole
    Larson and Mary Story, *Menu Labeling: Does Providing
    Nutrition Information at the Point of Purchase Affect
    Consumer Behavior?* (Robert Wood Johnson Foundation,
    June 2009).
40 Broadcasting Commission of Ireland, 'Children's Advertising
    Code', www.bci.ie, 4 June 2013; Elisabeth Rosenthal, 'Europe
    Takes Aim at Junk Food Ads', *New York Times*, www.nytimes.
    com, 6 January 2005.
41 Jenna Birch, 'Should Fast Food Labels Have Warnings Similar
    to Cigarettes?', www.yahoo.com, 23 March 2015.

4 MARKETING

1 Lisa M. Powell, Binh T. Nguyen and Euna Han, 'Energy
   Intake from Restaurants: Demographics and Socioeconomics,
   2003–2008', *American Journal of Preventive Medicine*, XLIII/5
   (November 2012), pp. 498–504.
2 J. L. Harris, M. B. Schwartz, K. D. Brownell et al., 'Fast Food
   F.A.C.T.S.: Evaluating Fast Food Nutrition and Marketing
   to Youth', Rudd Center for Food Policy and Obesity,
   www.fastfoodmarketing.org, November 2013.
3 Mindy F. Ji, 'Children's Relationships with Brands: "True Love"
   or "One-night" Stand?', *Psychology and Marketing*, XIX/2 (April
   2002), pp. 369–87.

4   Quoted in Kevin Short, 'Fast Food Marketing Disproportionately Targets Kids in Black Neighborhoods: Study', Huffington Post, www.huffingtonpost.com, 12 November 2014.

5   *Joint WHO/FAO Expert Consultation on Diet, Nutrition and the Prevention of Chronic Diseases,* WHO Technical Report Series 916 (World Health Organization, 2003).

6   Harris et al., 'Fast Food F.A.C.T.S.'

7   Quoted in Physicians Committee for Responsible Medicine, 'McDonald's, Wendy's Top List of Five Worst Fast-food Kids Meals', www.pcrm.org, 25 August 2010.

8   McDonald's, www.aboutmcdonalds.com, accessed 17 March 2015.

9   National Restaurant Association, 'Industry Impact', www.restaurant.org, accessed 1 May 2015.

10 Center for Science in the Public Interest, 'Class Action Lawsuit Targets McDonald's Use of Toys to Market to Children', www.cspinet.org, 15 December 2010.

11 Center for Science in the Public Interest, 'Obesity on the Kids' Menus at Top Chains', www.cspinet.org, August 2008.

12 Center for Science in the Public Interest, 'Kids' Meals II: Obesity and Poor Nutrition on the Menu', www.cspinet.org, 2013.

13 Consensus Action on Salt and Health, 'New Survey Names and Shames UK's "Saltiest" Family-friendly Eateries and Warns of a New Generation of "Salt Addicts"', www.actiononsalt.org.uk, 12 March 2015.

14 *Kids and Moms Consumer Trend Report* (Technomic Information Services, 2009).

15 Ashton Edwards, 'Fast Food Chain Recalling Kid's Meal Toys for Safety Hazard', Fox 13, www.fox13now.com, 10 November 2014.

16 Maureen Morrison, 'Just How Happy Does the Happy Meal Make McDonald's?', *Advertising Age*, www.adage.com, 29 November 2010.

17 Federal Trade Commission, *Marketing Food to Children: A Review of Industry . . . Activities, and Self-regulation: Report to Congress,* July 2008, p. ES-3.

18 A. M. Bernhardt et al., 'How Television Fast Food Marketing Aimed at Children Compares with Adult Advertisements', *PLOS ONE*, www.rwjf.org, 13 August 2013.

19 Julian E. Barnes, 'Fast-food Giveaway Toys Face Rising Recalls', *New York Times*, www.nytimes.com, 16 August 2001.

20 Jennifer Curtis, 'McDonald's Attacked for Toys that Push its Fatty Fast Food', *West Australian* (Perth), 16 January 2007.
21 Quoted in Rachel Gordon, 'Mayor Gavin Newsom Vetoes Fast-food Toy Ban', SFGate, www.sfgate.com, 13 November 2010.
22 Fox News Latino, 'Chile Bans Toys in Fast Food to Attack Child Obesity', www.latino.foxnews.com, 2 August 2012.
23 Livia Gamble, 'Should Australia Ban Fast Food Toys?', *Essential Kids*, www.essentialkids.com.au, 27 August 2014.
24 Dominic Green, 'Here Are All the People Plotting to Kill the McDonald's Happy Meal', *Business Insider*, www.businessinsider.com, 25 April 2013.
25 Ruth Hill, 'Burger King Bins Toys: Far Enough?', *Radio New Zealand*, www.radionz.co.nz, 17 April 2015.
26 Quoted in LawInfo Blog, 'Class Action Lawsuit Against Happy Meals is Dismissed', www.blog.lawinfo.com, accessed 1 May 2015.
27 L. Craypo et al., 'Fast Food Sales on High School Campuses: Results from the 2000 California High School Fast Food Survey', *Journal of School Health*, LXII (2002), pp. 78–82.
28 Jennifer L. Harris and Tracy Fox, 'Food and Beverage Marketing in Schools: Putting Student Health at the Head of the Class', Rudd Center for Food Policy and Obesity, www.uconnrudd-center.org, 13 January 2014.
29 Shellie Deringer, 'Limeades for Learning: Earn $450 for your Classroom', We Are Teachers, www.weareteachers.com, accessed 1 May 2015.
30 J. E. Brand and S. Greenberg, 'Commercials in the Classroom: The Impact of Channel One Advertising', *Journal of Advertising Research*, XXXIV (1994), pp. 18–27.
31 Evelyn Long, 'Annual McStaff Night Fun for All', *Morrow County Sentinel*, www.morrowcountysentinel.com, 12 March 2015.
32 H. Wechsler et al., 'Food Service and Foods and Beverages Available at School: Results from the School Health Policies and Programs Study 2000', *Journal of School Health*, LXXI (2001), pp. 313–24; Deborah Lehmann, 'Why School Cafeterias Are Dishing Out Fast Food', Education.com, 21 October 2013.
33 Yvonne M. Terry-McElrath et al., 'Commercialism in U.S. Elementary and Secondary School Nutrition Environments, Trends from 2007 to 2012', *JAMA Pediatrics*, CLXXX/3 (2014), pp. 234–42.

34 S. Bryn Austin et al., 'Clustering of Fast-food Restaurants around Schools', *American Journal of Public Health*, xcv/9 (2005), pp. 1575–81.

35 Janet M. Currie et al., 'The Effect of Fast Food Restaurants on Obesity', *American Economic Journal: Economic Policy*, xx/3 (August 2010), pp. 32–63.

36 Cara Buckley, 'A Proposal to Separate Fast Food and Schools', *New York Times*, www.nytimes.com, 19 April 2009.

37 H. Nixon and L. Doud, 'Do Fast Food Restaurants Cluster Around High Schools? A Geospatial Analysis of Proximity of Fast Food Restaurants to High Schools and the Connection to Childhood Obesity Rates', *Journal of Agriculture, Food Systems, and Community Development*, xxi (2011), pp. 181–94.

38 Brennan Davis and Christopher Carpenter, 'Proximity of Fast-food Restaurants to Schools and Adolescent Obesity', *American Journal of Public Health*, xcix (March 2009), pp. 505–10.

39 Kelly M. Purtell and Elizabeth T. Gershoff, 'Fast Food Consumption and Academic Growth in Late Childhood', *Clinical Pediatrics*, www.cpj.sagepub.com, 5 December 2014.

40 McDonald's uk, www.mcdonalds.com, accessed 1 May 2015.

41 Quoted in Obesity Policy Coalition, 'McDonald's Slammed for Offering Cash Rebates to Schools When Students Buy Fast Food', www.opc.org.au, 17 February 2015.

42 Lindsey Tanner, 'Pediatric Hospitals that Serve Fast Food Raise More Alarm', *Chron*, www.chron.com, 28 December 2006.

43 Yahoo Food, 'Doctors Fight to Ban Fast Food from Hospitals – and for Good Reason', www.yahoo.com, 3 March 2015.

44 Aseem Malhotra, 'It's Time to Ban Junk Food on Hospital Premises', *British Medical Journal*, cccxlvi (June 2013), p. f3932; Denis Campbell, 'Ban Fast-food Outlets from Hospitals, mps Demand', *The Guardian*, www.theguardian.com, 24 March 2015.

45 Bernhardt et al., 'How Television Fast Food Marketing Aimed at Children Compares with Adult Advertisements'.

46 Morrison, 'Just How Happy Does the Happy Meal Make McDonald's?'

47 'Children's Educational Television', Federal Communication Commission, www.fcc.gov, accessed 1 May 2015.

48 D. F. Roberts, U. G. Foehr and V. Rideout, *Generation M: Media in the Lives of 8–18-year-olds* (Kaiser Family Foundation, March 2005).

49 Erik Landhuis et al., 'Programming Obesity and Poor Fitness: The Long-term Impact of Childhood Television', *Obesity*, XVI (2008), pp. 1457–9; T. J. Parsons, O. Manor and C. Power, 'Television Viewing and Obesity: A Prospective Study in the 1958 British Birth Cohort', *European Journal of Clinical Nutrition*, LXII (2008), pp. 1355–63.

50 Better Business Bureau, 'Children's Food and Beverage Advertising Initiative', www.bbb.org, accessed 1 May 2015.

51 Rudd Center for Food Policy and Obesity, 'Evaluating Fast Food Nutrition and Marketing to Youth', www.rwjf.org, November 2010.

52 Rudd Center for Food Policy and Obesity, 'Fast-food Television Ads Use Toys, Movies to Target Kids', www.rwjf.org, 28 August 2013.

53 A. M. Bernhardt et al., 'Children's Recall of Fast Food Television Advertising: Testing the Adequacy of Food Marketing Regulation', *PLOS ONE*, www.journals.plos.org, 4 March 2015.

54 Michael Grossman, Erdal Tekin and Roy Wada, 'Fast-food Restaurant Advertising on Television and its Influence on Youth Body Composition', National Bureau of Economic Research, www.papers.nber.org, December 2012.

55 Hill, 'Burger King Bins Toys'.

56 'KFC Fun Crew!', www.datamart-tt.com, accessed 1 May 2015.

57 Amanda Lenhart et al., *Social Media and Mobile Internet Use Among Teens and Young Adults*, PewInternet, www.pewinternet. org, 3 February 2010.

58 Harris et al., 'Fast Food F.A.C.T.S.'

59 'Wendy's and Pizza Hut Are Crowned the Top Quick Service Restaurant Brands on Social Media', *Market Watch*, www. marketwatch.com, 7 April 2015.

60 Angela Doland, 'How KFC Reinvented the Fast Food Toy Meal in China; Ogilvy Shanghai Created a Mobile App for the Promo that Got 1.3 Million Downloads in a Month', *Advertising Age*, www.adage.com, 6 February 2015.

61 Robert Hof, 'Once Again, Starbucks Shows Google and Apple How to Do Mobile Payment', Forbes, www.forbes.com, 22 January 2015.

62 Lucas Peterson, 'Burger King Now Advertising with Something Called "Tittygram"', Eater UK, www.eater.com, 24 April 2015.

63 *The Scarecrow* video, YouTube, www.youtube.com, accessed 1 May 2015.

64 'Pizza Hut Celebrates Successful Delivery to Space', Space.com, www.space.com, 22 May 2001.

65 The Subservient Chicken, www.subservientchicken.com, accessed 1 May 2015.

66 *Happy Meal* video, YouTube, www.youtube.com, accessed 1 May 2015.

67 'Italian Pizza Chefs Threaten Legal Action over McDonald's Advert Claiming Children Prefer Hamburgers', *The Telegraph*, www.telegraph.co.uk, 12 April 2015.

68 Kashmir Hill, '#McDStories: When a Hashtag Becomes a Bashtag', Forbes, www.forbes.com, 24 January 2012.

69 Michael Walsh, 'Taco Bell Does Damage Control after Employee Caught Licking Shells', *New York Daily News*, www.nydailynews.com, 5 June 2013.

70 Quoted in Madison Park, 'Group Tells Ronald McDonald to Take a Hike', *The Chart*, www.thechart.blogs.cnn.com, 30 March 2010.

71 Megan Gibson, 'Ronald McDonald Beheaded: Finnish Activists Capture Fast-food Icon', *Time*, www.newsfeed.time.com, 16 February 2011.

72 Harris et al., 'Fast Food F.A.C.T.S.'

73 Quoted in Maria Godoy, 'Catcher in the Fry? McDonald's Happy Meals with a Side of Books', National Public Radio, www.npr.org, 10 October 2013.

74 Broadcasting Commission of Ireland, 'Children's Advertising Code', www.bci.ie, 4 June 2013.

75 Tirtha Dhar and Kathy Baylis, 'Fast-food Consumption and the Ban on Advertising Targeting Children: The Quebec Experience', *Journal of Marketing Research*, XLVIII/5 (October 2011), pp. 799–813.

76 'HFSS Advertising Restrictions: Final Review', Stakeholders. Ofcom, www.stakeholders.ofcom.org.uk, 26 July 2010.

77 Grossman, Tekin and Wada, 'Fast-food Restaurant Advertising on Television'.

78 Harris et al., 'Fast Food F.A.C.T.S.'

79 S. C. Duerksen et al., 'Family Restaurant Choices Are Associated with Child and Adult Overweight Status in Mexican-American

Families', *Journal of the American Dietetic Association*, CVII (2007), pp. 849–53.

80 Punam Ohri-Vachaspati et al., 'Child-directed Marketing Inside and on the Exterior of Fast Food Restaurants', *American Journal of Preventive Medicine*, XLVIII/1 (January 2015), pp. 22–30.

81 Harris et al., 'Fast Food F.A.C.T.S.'

82 George Ritzer, *The Globalization of Nothing 2* (Thousand Oaks, CA, 2007), p. 154.

83 Colin D. Rehm and Adam Drewnowski, 'Trends in Energy Intakes by Type of Fast Food Restaurant Among U.S. Children from 2003 to 2010', *JAMA Pediatrics* (30 March 2015), p. E1.

84 'Better Deals and More Sophisticated Palates Contribute to Kids Meals Decline, Reports NPD', NDP Group, www.npd.com, 22 May 2012.

5 ENVIRONMENT

1 McSpotlight, 'What's Wrong with McDonald's?', www.mcspotlight.org, accessed 1 May 2015.

2 Terence Chea, 'Oakland Wants Takeout Tax to Pay for Litter Clean-up', *USA Today*, www.usatoday30.usatoday.com, 6 February 2006; and Kiera Butler, 'Fast Food's Litter Legacy', *Mother Jones*, www.motherjones.com, 27 June 2011.

3 McDonald's, 'Global Best of Green 2012', www.aboutmcdonalds.com, accessed 1 May 2015.

4 Mike Roselle, 'Burger King Protest Set', *Earth First! Journal*, 20 March 1984.

5 K. Aronoff, 'U.S. Activists Stop Burger King from Importing Rainforest Beef', Global Nonviolent Action, www.nvdatabase.swarthmore.edu, 18 September 2011.

6 Greenpeace, 'McDonald's Pledges to Help Protect the Amazon', www.greenpeace.org, 26 July 2006.

7 Union of Concerned Scientists, 'Fries, Face Wash, Forests: Scoring America's Top Brands on the Palm Oil Commitments', www.ucsusa.org, April 2015.

8 Sonia van Gilder Cooke, 'Why Going Green Can Mean Big Money for Fast-food Chains', *Time*, www.time.com, 9 April 2012.

9 'McDonald's and Environmental Defense Fund Mark 20 Years of Partnerships for Sustainability', www.edf.org, 15 November 2012.

10 Anne Marie Mohan, 'KFC's Sustainable Sides Container Is "Sogood",
    Greener Package, www.greenerpackage.com, accessed 1 May 2015.
11 Guy Pearse, *Greenwash: Big Brands and Carbon Scams*
    (Collingwood, VIC, Australia, 2012).

6 MEAT

1   Eric Schlosser, *Fast Food Nation: The Dark Side of the
    All-American Meal* (New York, 2012), p. 6.
2   Ibid., p. 272.
3   Human Rights Watch Report, 'Blood, Sweat, and Fear: Workers'
    Rights in U.S. Meat and Poultry Plants', www.hrw.org, January
    2005.
4   Robert Paarlberg, *Food Politics: What Everyone Needs to Know*,
    2nd edn (New York, 2013), p. 157.
5   Laurence S. Shore and Amy Pruden, eds, *Hormones and
    Pharmaceuticals Generated by Concentrated Animal Feeding
    Operations: Transport in Water and Soil* (New York, 2009),
    pp. 5, 114.
6   Danielle Nierenberg, *State of the World 2006: A Worldwatch
    Institute Report on Progress Toward a Sustainable Society*
    (New York, 2006), p. 26.
7   Maureen Ogle, *In Meat We Trust: An Unexpected History
    of Carnivore America* (Boston, MA, 2013), p. 111.
8   Ron Barrett and George Armelagos, *An Unnatural History
    of Emerging Infections* (New York, 2013), p. 104.
9   Humane Society of the United States, 'Human Health
    Implications of Non-Therapeutic Antibiotic Use in Animal
    Agriculture', www.humanesociety.org, accessed 1 May 2015.
10 'McDonald's Outlines New Chicken Policy but Experts Point to
    Failed Promises', *The Guardian*, www.theguardian.com, 4 March
    2015.
11 Peter Salisbury, 'Behind the Brand: McDonald's', *The Ecologist*,
    www.theecologist.org, 16 June 2011; and McDonald's, www.
    mcdonalds.com, accessed 1 May 2015.
12 People for the Ethical Treatment of Animals, 'PETA's History:
    Compassion in Action', www.peta.org, accessed 1 May 2015.
13 *Pilgrim's Pride* video, YouTube, www.youtube.com, accessed
    2 May 2015.

14 'Pamela Anderson Writes to KFC Korea', *Seoul Times*, www.
theseoultimes.com, accessed 1 May 2015.

15 Quoted in Karin Bennett, 'Andy Dick Makes for a Frighteningly
Realistic "Ronald McDonald"', www.peta.org, 17 June 2009.

16 Julie Jargon, 'New Ad Targets McDonald's', *Wall Street Journal*,
www.wsj.com, 14 September 2010.

17 Andrew Campa, 'Customers Today Are Not Lovin' McDonald's',
Daily Titan, www.dailytitan.com, 16 March 2015.

18 McDonald's, www.mcdonalds.com, accessed 1 May 2015.

19 'Child and Consumer Advocates Urge FTC to Investigate and Bring
Action Against Google for Excessive and Deceptive Advertising
Aimed at Children', PRNewswire, www.prnewswire.com, 7 April
2015.

20 Tina Volpe, *The Fast Food Craze: Wreaking Havoc on our
Bodies and our Animals* (Kagel Canyon, CA, 2005), p. 5;
Jeff Nelson, 'McDonald's Settlement: A Study in Greed,
Corruption – and Heroism', VegSource, www.vegsource.com,
5 February 2003.

21 Francine Grace, 'McDonald's Settles Beef over Fries', CBS *News*,
www.cbsnews.com, 5 June 2002.

22 L. V. Anderson, 'Taco Bell's Seasoned Meat is Only 88 Percent
Beef: It Should Be Way, Way Less', Slate, www.slate.com,
1 May 2014.

23 Jonathan Stempel, 'Taco Bell Lawsuit Dropped after Dismissal
by Plaintiff', *Christian Science Monitor*, www.csmonitor.com,
19 April 2011.

24 Brigid Prayson et al. 'Fast Food Hamburgers: What Are We
Really Eating?', *Annals of Diagnostic Pathology*, XII/6 (December
2008), pp. 406–9.

25 In New York City, an Egyptian American street vendor launched
'Halal Guys' in 1990. While not a fast-food chain, it has expanded
into additional carts and storefronts in the city, and has plans to
expand to other states.

26 Edward Cody, 'Letter from France: Hamburger Chain's Decision
Sparks Tensions over Islam', *Washington Post*,
www.washingtonpost.com, 13 October 2010.

27 Abul Taher, 'Chicken McHalal: McDonald's Denied Using Halal
Meat; Now It Admits Meat Is in One of its Most Popular Meals',
Daily Mail, www.dailymail.co.uk, 9 October 2010.

28 Niraj Warikoo, 'McDonald's Drops Halal Food from u.s. Menu',
    USA Today, www.usatoday.com, 24 June 2013.
29 'Meat Production Continues to Rise', World Watch Institute,
    www.worldwatch.org, accessed 1 May 2015.
30 'u.s. Is Ahead of Europe in Slaughtering Plants', *Veterinary
    Ireland Journal*, III/5 (May 2013), p. 224.
31 Harvey Blatt, *America's Food: What You Don't Know About What
    You Eat* (Boston, MA, 2011), p. 259.

7 LABOUR

1   The Unhived Mind, 'Fast Food Workers Protest in 236 U.S. Cities',
    www.theunhivedmind.com, 15 April 2015; Bruce Horovitz and
    Yamiche Alcindor, 'Fast-food Strikes Widen into Social-justice
    Movement', *USA Today*, www.usatoday.com, 15 April 2015.
2   Annalyn Kurtz, 'Subway Leads Fast Food Industry in Underpaying
    Workers', CNN Money, www.money.cnn.com, 1 May 2014.
3   Cameron Lynne Macdonald and Carmen Sirianni, eds, *Working
    in the Service Society* (Philadelphia, PA, 1996).
4   Erik Forman, 'Fast Food Unionism: The Unionization
    of McDonald's and/or the McDonaldization of Unions',
    Recomposition, www.recomposition.info, 15 November 2013.
5   John Atlas, *Seeds of Change: The Story of Acorn, America's
    Most Controversial Antipoverty Community Organizing Group*
    (Nashville, TN, 2010), pp. 54–5.
6   Tiffany Hsu, 'Nearly 90% of Fast-food Workers Allege Wage
    Theft, Survey Finds', *LA Times*, www.latimes.com, 1 April 2015.
7   Tony Royle, *Working for McDonald's in Europe: The Unequal
    Struggle?* (New York, 2001), p. 103.
8   Inquisitr, 'Burger King Closes 89 Stores in Germany Due to
    Scandal', www.inquisitr.com, 24 November 2014.
9   'Fast Food Wage Scandal in S. China', www.china.org.cn,
    accessed 2 May 2015.
10 Sylvia A. Allegretto et al., 'Fast Food, Poverty Wages: The Public
    Cost of Low-Wage Jobs in the Fast-food Industry', Labor Center,
    University of California at Berkeley, www.laborcenter.berkeley.
    edu, 15 October 2013.
11 Michael B. Sauter, Thomas C. Frohlich and Alexander E. M.
    Hess, 'Fast-food Chains Costing Taxpayers the Most Money',

24/7 Wall St, www.247wallst.com, 21 October 2013.

12 Susan Berfield, 'Fast-food Wages Come with a $7 Billion Side of Public Assistance', Bloomberg, www.bloomberg.com, 15 October 2013.

13 Ken Jacobs, Ian Perry and Jenifer MacGillvary, 'The High Public Cost of Low Wages', Labor Center, University of California at Berkeley, www.laborcenter.berkeley.edu, April 2015.

14 Jillian Berman, 'It Takes a McDonald's Worker 4 Months to Earn What the CEO Gets in an Hour', Huffington Post, www.huffingtonpost.com, 10 December 2013.

15 Steven Greenhouse, 'Wage Strikes Planned at Fast-food Outlets', *New York Times*, www.nytimes.com, 1 December 2013.

16 Georgina Cairns et al., 'Systematic Reviews of the Evidence on the Nature, Extent and Effects of Food Marketing to Children: A Retrospective Summary', *Appetite*, LXII (2012), pp. 209–15.

17 National Labor Relations Board, 'NLRB Office of the General Counsel Issues Consolidated Complaints Against McDonald's Franchisees and their Franchisor McDonald's, USA, LLC as Joint Employers', www.nlrb.gov, 19 December 2014.

18 Quoted in William Finnegan, 'Dignity: Fast-food Workers and a New Form of Labor Activism', *New Yorker*, www.newyorker.com, 15 September 2015.

19 Eric Schlosser, 'How to Make the Country's Most Dangerous Job Safer', *The Atlantic Monthly*, CCLXXXIX (January 2002), p. 34.

20 'Key Findings from a Survey on Fast Food Worker Safety', Huffington Post, www.huffingtonpost.com, 16 March 2015.

21 'Unions Set to Take on Fast Food Giants Over Low Pay', *The Herald*, www.heraldscotland.com, 16 November 2014.

22 Tim Bell, 'Pictures: "End Zero Hour Contracts!": McDonald's Staff Stand in Solidarity', TVNZ, www.tvnz.co.nz, 15 April 2015.

23 Eric Schlosser, *Fast Food Nation: The Dark Side of the All-American Meal* (New York, 2001), p. 233.

24 Liz Alderman and Steven Greenhouse, 'Living Wages, Rarity for U.S. Fast-food Workers, Served Up in Denmark', *New York Times*, www.nytimes.com, 27 October 2014.

25 Royle, *Working for McDonald's in Europe*, p. 205.

26 Ibid., p. 171.

27 Michelle Chen, 'Five Myths about Fast-food Work', *Washington Post*, www.washingtonpost.com, 17 April 2015; Kevin Short,

'Working at McDonald's is Starkly Different in These 3 Countries', Huffington Post, www.huffingtonpost.com, 15 May 2014.

28 Quoted in Bill Hutchinson, 'McDonald's Will Raise Wages of 90,000 Employees by 10 Percent', *Daily News*, www.nydailynews. com, 2 April 2015.

29 'A Look at the College Tuition Perks at Starbucks, McDonald's', AOL Jobs, www.jobs.aol.com, 7 April 2014.

BIBLIOGRAPHY

GENERAL

Bishop, Marlene R., ed., *Chocolate, Fast Foods, and Sweeteners: Consumption and Health* (New York, 2010)

Bové, José, François Dufour and Gilles Luneau, *The World Is Not for Sale: Farmers Against Junk Food* (New York, 2001)

Brownell, Kelly D., and Katherine Battle Horgen, *Food Fight: The Inside Story of the Food Industry, America's Obesity Crisis, and What We Can Do about It* (Chicago, IL, 2004)

Cairns, Georgina, Kathryn Angus and Gerard Hastings, *The Extent, Nature and Effects of Food Promotion to Children: A Review of the Evidence to December 2008* (Geneva, 2009)

Cohon, George, *To Russia with Fries* (Toronto, 1997)

Conza, Tony, *Success: It's a Beautiful Thing: Lessons on Life and Business from the Founder of Blimpie International* (New York, 2000)

Emerson, Robert L., *Fast Food: The Endless Shakeout* (New York, 1979)

Federal Trade Commission, *Marketing Food to Children and Adolescents: A Review of Industry Expenditures, Activities and Self-regulation* (Washington, DC, 2008)

Franz, Marion J., *Fast Food Facts: Nutritive and Exchange Values for Fast-food Restaurants* (Minneapolis, MN, 1983)

Hamrick, Karen S., and Abigail M. Okrent, *The Role of Time in Fast-food Behavior in the United States* (Washington, DC, 2014)

Hawkes, Corinna, *Marketing Food to Children: The Global Regulatory Environment* (Geneva, 2004)

Healey, Justin, ed., *Fast Food* (Thirroul, NSW, Australia, 2012)

Hogan, David Gerald, *Selling 'em by the Sack: White Castle and the Creation of American Food* (New York, 1997)

Ingram, Billy, *All This from a 5-cent Hamburger! The Story of the White Castle System* (New York, 1964)

Jacobson, Michael F., and Sarah Fritschner, *The Fast-Food Guide: What's Good, What's Bad, and How to Tell the Difference*, 2nd edn (New York, 1991)

Jakle, John A., and Keith A. Sculle, *Fast Food: Roadside Restaurants in the Automobile Age* (Baltimore, MD, 1999)

Karcher, Carl, and B. Carolyn Knight, *Never Stop Dreaming: The Story of Carl Karcher Enterprises* (San Marcos, CA, 1991)

Kessler, David A., *The End of Overeating: Taking Control of the Insatiable American Appetite* (New York, 2009)

Kroc, Ray, with Robert Anderson, *Grinding It Out: The Making of McDonald's* (Chicago, IL, 1977)

Kuisel, Richard F., *The French Way: How France Embraced and Rejected American Values and Power* (Princeton, NJ, 2012)

Liu, Warren, *KFC in China: Secret Recipe for Success* (Singapore and Hoboken, NJ, 2008)

Love, John F., *McDonald's Behind the Arches* (New York, 1995)

Lynd, Staughton, and Daniel Gross, *Solidarity Unionism at Starbucks* (Oakland, CA, 2011)

McGinnis, J. Michael, Jennifer Appleton Gootman and Vivica I. Kraak, *Food Marketing to Children and Youth: Threat or Opportunity?*, Institute of Medicine's Committee on Food Marketing and the Diets of Children and Youth (Washington, DC, 2006)

McLamore, James W., *The Burger King: Jim McLamore and the Building of an Empire* (New York, 1998)

Mander, Jerry, and Edward Goldsmith, eds, *The Case Against the Global Economy: And For a Turn Toward the Local* (San Francisco, CA, 1996)

Monaghan, Tom, with Robert Anderson, *Pizza Tiger* (New York, 1986)

Moss, Michael, *Salt Sugar Fat: How the Food Giants Hooked Us* (New York, 2013)

Nierenberg, Danielle, *Happier Meals: Rethinking the Global Meat Industry* (Washington, DC, 2005)

Otis, Caroline H., et al., *The Cone with the Curl on Top: Celebrating Fifty Years, 1940–1990* (Minneapolis, MN, 1990)

Ozersky, Josh, *Hamburgers: A Cultural History* (New Haven, CT, 2008)

Parsa, H. G., and Francis A. Kwansa, eds, *Quick Service Restaurants, Franchising, and Multi-unit Chain Management* (New York, 2002)

Perl, Lila, *Junk Food, Fast Food, Health Food: What America Eats and Why* (New York, 1980)

Perman, Stacy, *In-N-Out Burger: A Behind-the-Counter Look at the Fast-Food Chain that Breaks All the Rules* (New York, 2009)

Reiter, Ester, *Making Fast Food: From the Frying Pan into the Fryer* (Montreal and Kingston, Canada, 1991)

Ritzer, George, *Explorations in the Sociology of Consumption: Fast Food, Credit Cards and Casinos* (London and Thousand Oaks, CA, 2001)

—, *The Globalization of Nothing 2* (Thousand Oaks, CA, 2007)

—, *The McDonaldization of Society*, revd edn (Thousand Oaks, CA, 1996)

—, *The McDonaldization of Society*, 8th edn (London and Thousand Oaks, CA, 2015)

Royle, Tony, *Working for McDonald's in Europe: The Unequal Struggle?* (New York, 2001)

—, and Brian Towers, eds, *Labour Relations in the Global Fast Food Industry* (New York, 2002)

Sanders, Harland, *Life as I Have Known It has been Finger Lickin' Good* (Carol Stream, IL, 1974)

Schlosser, Eric, *Fast Food Nation: The Dark Side of the All-American Meal* (New York, 2001)

—, and Charles Wilson, *Chew On This: Everything You Don't Want to Know about Fast Food* (Boston, MA, 2006)

Smith, Andrew F., *Hamburger: A Global History* (London, 2008)

—, *Junk Food and Fast Food: An Encyclopedia of What We Love to Eat*, 2nd edn, 2 vols (Santa Barbara, CA, 2012)

—, *Potato: A Global History* (London, 2011)

Spurlock, Morgan, *Don't Eat this Book: Fast Food and the Supersizing of America* (New York, 2005)

Talwar, Jennifer Parker, *Fast Food, Fast Track: Immigrants, Big Business, and the American Dream* (Boulder, CO, 2002)

Tannock, Stuart, *Youth at Work: The Unionized Fast-food and Grocery Workplace* (Philadelphia, PA, 2001)

Thomas, R. David, *Dave's Way: A New Approach to Old-fashioned Success* (New York, 1991)

Thorner, Marvin Edward, *Convenience and Fast Food Handbook* (Westport, CT, 1973)

Vidal, John, *McLibel: Burger Culture on Trial* (New York, 1997)

Volpe, Tina, *The Fast Food Craze: Wreaking Havoc on our Bodies and our Animals* (Kagel Canyon, CA, 2005)

Waldman, Murray, and Marjorie Lamb, *Dying for a Hamburger: Modern Meat Processing and the Epidemic of Alzheimer's Disease* (New York, 2005)

Warshaw, Hope S., *Guide to Healthy Fast-food Eating* (Alexandria, VA, 2006)

Watson, James L., ed., *Golden Arches East: McDonald's in East Asia* (Stanford, CA, 1997)

ARTICLES

Abdollah, Tami, 'Limits Proposed on Fast-food Restaurants', *Los Angeles Times*, www.latimes.com, 10 September 2007

Adams, Ronald, 'Fast Food and Animal Rights: An Examination and Assessment of the Industry's Response to Social Pressure', *Business and Society Review*, CXIII/3 (September 2008), pp. 301–28

Bauer, Katherine W., et al., 'Energy Content of U.S. Fast-food Restaurant Offerings: 14-year Trends', *American Journal of Preventive Medicine*, XLIII/5 (November 2012), pp. 490–97

Belasco, Warren J., 'Ethnic Fast Foods: The Corporate Melting Pot', *Food and Foodways*, II/1 (April 1987), pp. 1–30

Bernhardt, A. M., et al., 'Children's Recall of Fast Food Television Advertising: Testing the Adequacy of Food Marketing Regulation', *PLOS ONE*, www.journals.plos.org, 4 March 2015

Block, J. P., R. A. Scribner and K. B. DeSalvo, 'Fast Food, Race, Ethnicity, and Income: A Geographic Analysis', *American Journal of Preventive Medicine*, XXVII/3 (2004), pp. 211–17

Bowman, S., and B. Vineyard, 'Fast Food Consumption of U.S. Adults: Impact on Energy and Nutrient Intakes and Overweight Status', *Journal of the American College of Nutrition*, XXIII/2 (2004), pp. 163–8

——, et al., 'Effects of Fast-Food Consumption on Energy Intake and Diet Quality Among Children in a National Household Survey', *Pediatrics*, CXIII/1 (1 January 2004), pp. 112–18

Burgoine, Thomas, et al., 'Associations Between Exposure to Takeaway Food Outlets, Takeaway Food Consumption, and Body Weight in Cambridgeshire, UK: Population Based, Cross Sectional Study', *British Medical Journal*, www.bmj.com, March 2014

Cairns, Georgina, et al., 'Systematic Reviews of the Evidence on the Nature, Extent and Effects of Food Marketing to Children: A Retrospective Summary', *Appetite*, LXII (2012), pp. 209–15

Cassey, Nell, 'Wage Theft and New York City's Fast Food Workers: New York City's Hidden Crime Wave', *Fast Food Foreword*, www.scribd.com, April 2013

Chou, Shin-Yi, I.A.S. Rashid and Michael Grossman, 'Fast-food Advertising on Television and its Influence on Childhood Obesity', *Journal of Law and Economics*, IV (2008), pp. 599–618

Consumer Reports, 'Where's the Beef?', *Consumer Reports* (July 1984), pp. 367–73

Currie, Janet M., et al., 'The Effect of Fast Food Restaurants on Obesity', *American Economic Journal: Economic Policy*, II/3 (August 2010), pp. 32–63

Dabelea, Dana, et al., 'Prevalence of Type 1 and Type 2 Diabetes Among Children and Adolescents from 2001 to 2009', *Journal of the American Medical Association*, CCCXI/17 (7 May 2014), pp. 1778–86

Davis, Brennan, and Christopher Carpenter, 'Proximity of Fast-food Restaurants to Schools and Adolescent Obesity', *American Journal of Public Health*, XCIX (March 2009), pp. 505–10

Duerksen, S. C., et al., 'Family Restaurant Choices are Associated with Child and Adult Overweight Status in Mexican-American Families', *Journal of the American Dietetic Association*, CVII (2007), pp. 849–53

Duffey, Kiyah J., Penny Gordon-Larsen, David R. Jacobs Jr, O. Dale Williams and Barry M. Popkin, 'Differential Associations of Fast Food and Restaurant Food Consumption with 3-y Change in Body Mass Index: The Coronary Artery Risk Development in Young Adults Study', *American Society for Clinical Nutrition*, LXXXV/1 (January 2007), pp. 201–8

Fantasia, Rick, 'Fast Food in France', *Theory and Society*, XXIV/2 (April 1995), pp. 201–43

Finnegan, William, 'Dignity: Fast-food Workers and a New Form of Labor Activism', *New Yorker*, www.newyorker.com, 15 September 2015

Finucane, Mariel M., 'National, Regional, and Global Trends in Body-mass Index since 1980: Systematic Analysis of Health

Examination Surveys and Epidemiological Studies with 960
    Country-years and 9.1 Million Participants', *The Lancet*, x (4
    February 2011), as at www.thelancet.com
Fleischhacker, S. E., et al., 'A Systematic Review of Fast Food Access
    Studies', *Obesity Review*, xii/5 (2011), pp. e460–e471
Food Empowerment Project, 'Fast Food', Food Empowerment
    Project, www.foodispower.org, accessed 1 May 2015
Forman, Erik, 'Fast Food Unionism: The Unionization of McDonald's
    and/or the McDonaldization of Unions', *Recomposition*,
    www.recomposition.info, 15 November 2013
Fragner, Bert, 'The Meyhane or McDonald's? Changes in Eating
    Habits and the Evolution of Fast Food in Istanbul', in *Culinary
    Cultures of the Middle East*, ed. Sami Zubaida and Richard
    Tapper (New York, 1994)
Freeman, Andrea, 'Fast Food: Oppression through Poor Nutrition',
    California Law Review, xcv/6 (December 2007), pp. 2221–59
French, S. A., L. Harnack and R. W. Jeffery, 'Fast Food Restaurant
    Use among Women in the Pound of Prevention Study: Dietary,
    Behavioral and Demographic Correlates', *International Journal of
    Obesity*, xxiv (October 2000), pp. 1353–9
Fryar, Cheryl D., and Ervin R. Bethene, 'Caloric Intake from Fast Food
    among Adults: United States, 2007–2010', www.cdc.gov, 2013
Gollain, Francoise, 'Anti-Globalisation Movements: Making and
    Reversing History', *Environmental Politics*, xi (Autumn 2002),
    pp. 164–7
Grossman, Michael, Erdal Tekin and Roy Wada, 'Fast-food
    Restaurant Advertising on Television and its Influence on Youth
    Body Composition', National Bureau of Economic Research,
    www.papers.nber.org, December 2012
Harris, Jennifer L., et al., 'Fast Food F.A.C.T.S.: Evaluating Fast Food
    Nutrition and Marketing to Youth', www.fastfoodmarketing.org,
    November 2010
Hawkes, C., 'Marketing Practices of Fast Food and Soft Drinks
    Multinationals: A Review', *Globalization, Diets, and
    Noncommunicable Diseases* (Geneva, 2002)
Jeffery, Robert, Judy Baxter, Mauree McGuire and Jennifer Linde,
    'Are Fast Food Restaurants an Environmental Risk Factor for
    Obesity?', *International Journal of Behavioral Nutrition and
    Physical Activity*, www.ijbnpa.org, 25 January 2006

Jekanowski, Mark D., James K. Binkley and James Eales, 'Convenience, Accessibility, and the Demand for Fast Food', *Journal of Agricultural and Resource Economics*, XXVI/1 (July 2001), pp. 58–74

Kelly, Bridget, et al., 'Television Food Advertising to Children: A Global Perspective', *American Journal of Public Health*, C (September 2010), pp. 1730–36

Kwate, N. O., 'Fried Chicken and Fresh Apples: Racial Segregation as a Fundamental Cause of Fast Food Density in Black Neighborhoods', *Health and Place*, XIV/1 (2008), pp. 32–44

Lau, Richard Curtis, 'Fast-food Consumption and the Fast-food Environment', Masters in Public Health thesis, University of Washington, 2012

McBride, Sarah, 'Exiling the Happy Meal', *Wall Street Journal*, www.wsj.com, 22 July 2008

Matejowsky, Ty, 'Fast Food and Nutritional Perceptions in the Age of "Globesity": Perspectives from the Provincial Philippines', *Food and Foodways*, XVII/1 (Spring 2009), pp. 29–49

—, 'Gender, Fast Food, and Nutritional Perspectives in the Contemporary Philippines', *Asia-Pacific Social Science Review*, X/1 (2010), pp. 1–20

—, 'Jolly Dogs and McSpaghetti: Anthropological Reflections on Global/Local Fast-food Competition in the Philippines', *Journal of Asia-Pacific Business*, IX/4 (2008), pp. 313–28

—, 'SPAM and Fast-food "Glocalization" in the Philippines', *Food, Culture and Society*, X/1 (2007), pp. 24–41

Mello, Michelle M., Eric B. Rimm and David M. Studdert, 'The McLawsuit: The Fast-food Industry and Legal Accountability for Obesity', *Health Affairs*, XXII/6 (November 2003), pp. 207–16

Mintz, Sidney, 'Afterward', in *Golden Arches East: McDonald's in East Asia*, ed. James L. Watson (Stanford, CA, 1997)

—, 'Fast Food Nation: What the All-American Meal is Doing to the World', *Times Literary Supplement* (14 September 2001), pp. 7–9

Niemeier, H. M., et al., 'Fast Food Consumption and Breakfast Skipping: Predictors of Weight Gain from Adolescence to Adulthood in a Nationally Representative Sample', *Journal of Adolescent Health*, XXXIX/6 (December 2006), pp. 842–9

Ohri-Vachaspati, Punam, et al., 'Child-Directed Marketing Inside
    and on the Exterior of Fast Food Restaurants', *American Journal
    of Preventive Medicine*, XLVIII/1 (January 2015), pp. 22–30
Olutayo, A. O., and O. Akanle, 'Fast Food in Ibadan: An Emerging
    Consumption Pattern', *Africa: Journal of the International African
    Institute*, LXXIX/2 (2009), pp. 207–27
Paeratakul S., et al., 'Fast-food Consumption among U.S. Adults and
    Children: Dietary and Nutrient Intake Profile', *American Dietary
    Association*, CIII/10 (October 2003), pp. 1332–8
Penfold, Steve, 'Selling by the Carload: The Early Years of Fast Food
    in Canada', in *Creating Postwar Canada: Community, Diversity,
    and Dissent, 1945–75*, ed. Magda Fahrni and Robert Rutherdale
    (Vancouver, 2008)
Pereira, M. A., et al., 'Fast-food Habits, Weight Gain, and Insulin
    Resistance (the Cardia Study): 15-year Prospective Analysis', *The
    Lancet*, CCCXCV (1 January 2005), pp. 36–42
Popkin, Barry M., 'The Public Health Implications of Fast-food
    Menu Labeling', *American Journal of Preventive Medicine*, XLIII/5
    (November 2012), pp. 569–70
Powell, Lisa M., Binh T. Nguyen and Euna Han, 'Energy Intake from
    Restaurants: Demographics and Socioeconomics, 2003–2008',
    American Journal of Preventive Medicine, XLIII/5 (November
    2012), pp. 498–504
Reiter, Ester, 'Fast-food in Canada Working Conditions, Labour
    Law and Unionization', in *Labour Relations in the Global Fast
    Food Industry*, ed. Tony Royle and Brian Towers (New York,
    2002)
Richards, Timothy J., Paul M. Patterson and Stephen F. Hamilton,
    'Fast Food, Addiction, and Market Power', *Journal of Agricultural
    and Resource Economics*, XXXII/3 (December 2007), pp. 425–47
—, and Luis Padilla, 'Promotion and Fast Food Demand', *American
    Journal of Agricultural Economics*, XCI/1 (February 2009),
    pp. 168–83
Richardson, A. S., et al., 'Neighborhood Fast Food Restaurants and
    Fast Food Consumption', *Public Health*, XI (July 2011), p. 543
Ross, Drew Eliot, 'Topography of Taste: Globalization, Cultural
    Politics, and the Making of California Cuisine', PhD thesis,
    University of Wisconsin-Madison, 1999
Rouhani, Mohammad Hossein, et al., 'Fast Food Consumption,

Quality of Diet, and Obesity among Isfahanian Adolescent Girls',
    Journal of Obesity, www.hindawi.com, 19 March 2012
Sallis, James F., and Karen Glanz, 'The Role of Built Environments in
    Physical Activity, Eating, and Obesity in Childhood', *The Future
    of Children*, XVI/1 (Spring 2006), pp. 89–108
Satia, J. A., et al., 'Eating at Fast-food Restaurants is Associated with
    Dietary Intake, Demographic, Psychosocial and Behavioural
    Factors among African Americans in North Carolina', *Public
    Health Nutrition*, VII/8 (December 2004), pp. 1089–96
Sharpe, Kathryn M., and Richard Staelin, 'Consumption Effects of
    Bundling: Consumer Perceptions, Firm Actions, and Public
    Policy Implications', *Journal of Public Policy and Marketing*,
    XXIX/2 (Fall 2010), pp. 170–88
Smith, Lee, 'Burger King Puts Down its Dukes', *Fortune* (16 June
    1980), pp. 90–97
Van Esterik, Penny, 'From Marco Polo to McDonald's: Thai Cuisine in
    Transition', *Food and Foodways*, V/2 (August 1992), pp. 177–93
Walshe, Sadhbh, 'How America's Fast Food Industry Makes a
    Quick Buck, the Gulf Between CEO Pay and Staff McWages
    is Shockingly Wide: A Strike Serves this System of Super-
    exploitation Right', *The Guardian*, www.theguardian.com, 10
    April 2013
Washi, Sidiga A., and Maha B. Ageib, 'Poor Diet Quality and Food
    Habits are Related to Impaired Nutritional Status in 13- to
    18-year-old Adolescents in Jeddah', *Nutrition Research*, XXX/8
    (2010), pp. 527–34
Yan, Yungxiang, 'Of Hamburger and Social Space', in *Food and
    Culture: A Reader*, ed. Carole Counihan and Penny Van Esterik,
    3rd edn (New York and London, 2012)
Young, Lisa R., and Marion Nestle, 'Portion Sizes and Obesity:
    Responses of Fast-food Companies', *Journal of Public Health
    Policy*, XXVIII/2 (2007), pp. 238–48
Yu, Er, 'Foreign Fast Foods Gobble Up Chinese-style Fast Foods',
    Chinese Sociology and Anthropology, XXXI (Summer 1999),
    pp. 80–87
Zhong, Chen-Bo, and Sanford E. DeVoe, 'You Are How You Eat:
    Fast Food and Impatience', *Psychological Science*, www.rotman.
    utoronto.ca, 19 March 2010

FILMS/DOCUMENTARIES

Fast Food Nation (dir. Richard Linklater, 2001), based on the book by
    Eric Schlosser (2001)
Food Chains (dir. Sanjay Rawal, 2015)
Food, Inc. (dir. Robert Kenner, 2008)
*Hamburger America: One Man's Cross-country Odyssey to Find the
    Best Burgers in the Nation* (dir. George Motz, 2008)
McLibel: Two People Who Wouldn't Say Sorry (dir. Franny Armstrong,
    2005)
Super Size Me (dir. Morgan Spurlock, 2004)

ORGANIZATIONS

Center for Science in the Public Interest (CSPI)
1875 Connecticut Avenue NW, Number 300
Washington, DC, 20009
+1 202 332 9110
www.cspinet.org

Greenpeace International
Ottho Heldringstraat 5
1066 AZ Amsterdam
The Netherlands
+31 (0) 20 718 20 00
+31 (0) 20 718 20 02
www.greenpeace.org/international/en

National Restaurant Association
1200 17th Street, NW
Washington, DC, 20036
+1 202 331 5900
www.restaurant.org

People for the Ethical Treatment of Animals (PETA)
501 Front Street
Norfolk, VA, 23510
www.peta.org

Physicians Committee for Responsible Medicine (PCRM)
5100 Wisconsin Avenue, NW, Suite 400,
Washington, DC, 20016
+1 202 686 2210
www.pcrm.org

Rainforest Action Network
www.ran.org

Rudd Center for Food Policy and Obesity
University of Connecticut
One Constitution Plaza
Suite 600
Hartford, CT, 06103
+1 860 380 1000
www.uconruddcenter.org

Slow Food International
Piazza XX Settembre, 5
12042 Bra (Cuneo), Italy
+39 0 172 419 611
www.slowfood.com

INDEX